WORLD WAR in CHARLEY

Charnwood's Hidden Parish

First published in Great Britain in 2009

The Charley Heritage Group

Hillside Bungalow, Abbey Road,

Coalville, Leicestershire LE 67 4UA

ISBN 978-0-9563579-0-8

Produced by members of the
Charley Heritage Group

Compiled by Terry Sheppard

A project funded by a grant from
Awards for All
A National Lottery Scheme

LOTTERY FUNDED

Published by the

Charley Heritage Group

Hillside Bungalow

Abbey Road, Coalville

Leicestershire LE67 4UA

The Charley Heritage Group in 2009:

Maureen & John Havers
David & Joyce Burton
Roger & Sandra Cooke
Sheila & Wilf Shelton
David & Kim Fitchett
Michael Froggatt
Terry Sheppard

Prepared in Serif Page Plus
in Baskerville BT 11pt

CONTENTS

ACKNOWLEDGEMENTS & SOURCES

The members of the Charley Heritage Group meet round a table from time to time and mostly talk heritage together with animation. Often a guest will join them with perhaps a box of photographs or other mementoes. Sometimes the tape recorder will come out and a fascinating story will be caught for posterity. At various times, members will be out and about on research forays, in the landscape, in record offices, at the Public Record Office at Kew, in reading books, and of course, on the Internet.

It is the fermentation in this productive pool that gave rise to this book. All the Compiler had to do was marshal it all together into a story.

Four books were of special help:

Dr R V Jones, *Most Secret War, British Scientific Intelligence, 1939-1945* Hamish Hamilton, London 1978.

Laurie Brettingham, *Royal Air Force Beambenders, No. 80 (Signals) Wing, 1940-1945*, Midland Publishing, Leicester 1997.

Austin J Ruddy, *To The Last Round, The Leicestershire and Rutland Home Guard, 1940-1945*, Breedon Books, Derby 2007.

Sadie Ward, *War in the Countryside 1939-1945,* Cameron Books, 1988.

The material on the National Farm Survey is lodged at the Public Record Office at Kew. The Maps under class MAF 73/22 Nos 24 & 27. The records in class MAF 32/379/135.

The microfilmed copies of the Loughborough Echo for the war years are kept at Loughborough Central Library.

We are grateful to those whose oral testimony appears in the book, especially Ken Nicholls JP and Dick Lovett, also to the Abbott at Mount St Bernard Abbey, for access to the Monastery Chronicle for the war years.

1 CHARLEY
The Hidden Heart of Charnwood Forest

Charley is a small civil parish nestling in the high places of Charnwood Forest. Turning off the A512 at Shepshed and following the road to Coalville brings the traveller over a first summit where the Forest area is laid out like a panorama. Negotiating the valley below, with eyes on the hill ahead, the driver may not notice that a small stream has been crossed. This is the Black Brook, feeding the reservoir of that name, and the boundary of Charley Parish. There are no proud or artistic roadside declarations of the name Charley, and the only clue might be the road name at the valley bottom, though for most of its length, outside the parish.

The sign at the bottom of the dip, just before the Blackbrook

Having ascended the hill from the Black Brook, and passing the staggered junction where the Oaks Road crosses, the driver may just notice the huge granite block on the left hand verge. The people of Charley had it placed here, emblazoned with the gilded legend Charley 2000, to let the world know that their delightful parish was alive in both the old and new millennia.

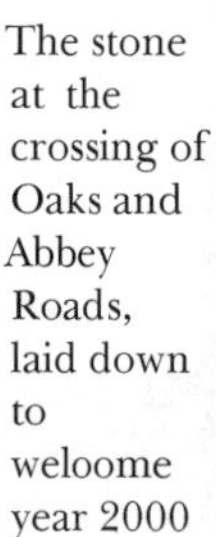

The stone at the crossing of Oaks and Abbey Roads, laid down to weloome year 2000

Less than a mile further on, just past High Tor Farm, is another summit, with urban Coalville in view below. This is the south western boundary of Charley. There went the parish, traversed in under two minutes.

Looking at the outline map on two following pages Charley Parish has a peculiar finger or toe jutting out of its north western edge, squeezing between the territory of Belton to the north, and Whitwick to the south. At the south eastern corner the boundary just crosses the M1 motorway at Copt Oak before swinging away down the Nanpantan Road. The good people of Charley made another mark on the landscape here at the Copt Oak corner by saving a parish pump from being lost to road works. It stands in its little bower, proclaiming its provenance to all who pass by.

The top of the Parish Pump preserved at Copt Oak Corner

Away up on the eastern end Charley Parish juts out to include Whittle Hill, looking down on Woodhouse one way, Loughborough another, and the forest incursion of Shepshed from the north.

---oo0Ooo----

Now listed as comprising 3,274 acres, and a population somewhere in the low 200s, it was not always so. Gaining and sometimes losing territory reflecting the history of local government reorganisation, Charley has a long provenance that includes a small entry in the Domesday Book of 1086. *Cernelega*, from the Celtic 'carn', a heap of stones, and the Old English 'leah', wood, or clearing in a wood. 'A woodland clearing among or near rocks and stones' about expresses the nature of the original Charley. The wild and secretive forest area, away from the productive lowland landscapes of the neighbouring manors, was ideal territory for the monastic ideal. The history of the resultant Charley Priory is not fully documented. After two centuries the Priory had run out of steam by 1465 and was merged into the nearby Augustinian Priory at Ulverscroft. Later and after the Reformation, the old enclosures made by Charley Priory from the wilderness became the retreat of the Bosworth family. At the centre was Charley Hall, and the enclosed land was worked by its two farms. If there was a place known as Charley in the 18th century, then it was Charley Hall and its farmland.

Charley Hall as drawn for the Charley Millennium Map

In 1808 the Lords of the surrounding manors had an Act of Parliament passed to "Enclose the Forest or Chase of Charnwood or Charley and Rothley Plain". The wilderness became the ordered and well-defined landscape we see today. The ancient enclosure around Charley Hall was recognised and not touched. Emerging from the Enclosure process was the eventual establishment of St James Church at The Oaks, in 1815, and

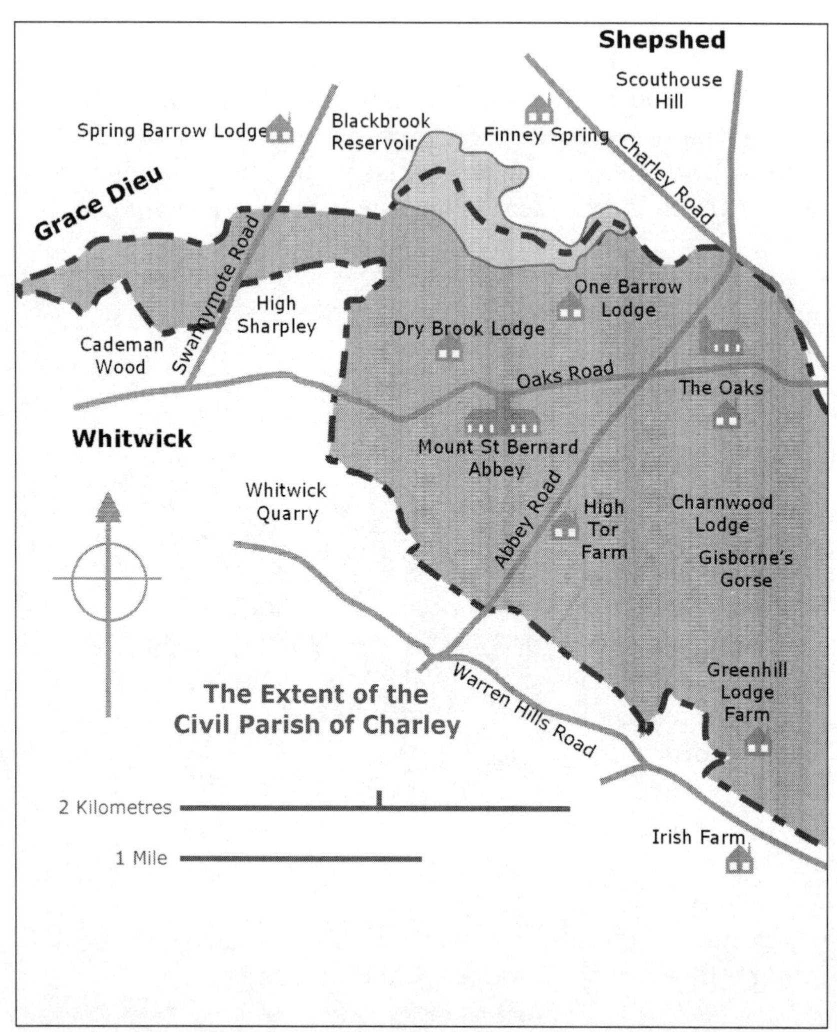

Schematic map of the western side of the civil Parish of Charley, hidden away on the high places of Charnwood Forest.

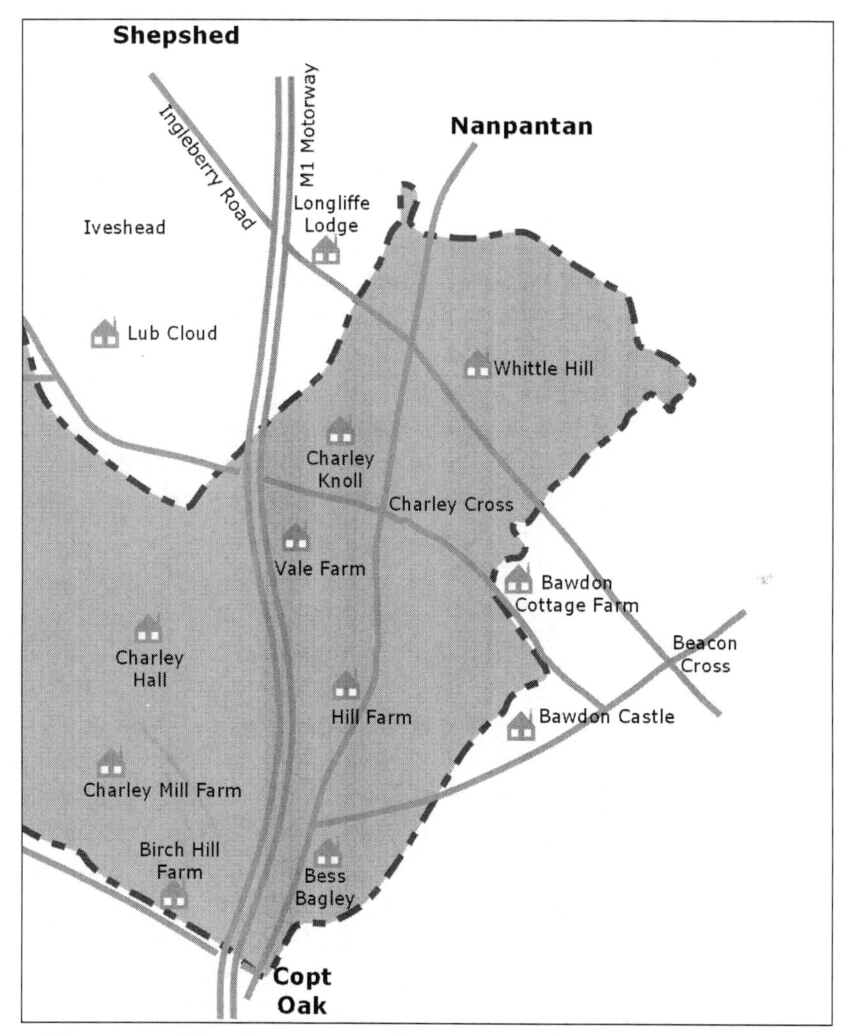

The eastern side, whose peace and quiet was mightily disturbed by the coming of the M1 Motorway.

St Peters at Copt Oak, in 1837. Later in mid century these had formal Ecclesiastical Districts assigned to them, reflecting their neighbouring lands.

By the end of the 19th century a formal structure of Councils at County and Rural District level had been put in place. Charley became an official Civil Parish in the Loughborough Rural District with an acreage of 1,334, and a population of around 150. A sensible territory around The Oaks Church was drawn, incorporating fingers of land from Newtown Linford and Markfield.

Data from Youngs, *Local Administrative Units: Northern England*, London, Royal Historical Society, 1991. P.223

In the 1936 round of local government reorganisation the size of Charley Civil Parish more than doubled to 3,274 acres. Parts of Woodhouse were incorporated in the east, and swathes of Whitwick in the west, when that ancient parish was subsumed into Coalville. In a quandary about where to put the enlarged Charley, the authorities placed it under the supervision of Castle Donington Rural District Council. Charley entered the war with a strange set of allegiances. Officially Castle Donington, but most ties being with Loughborough.

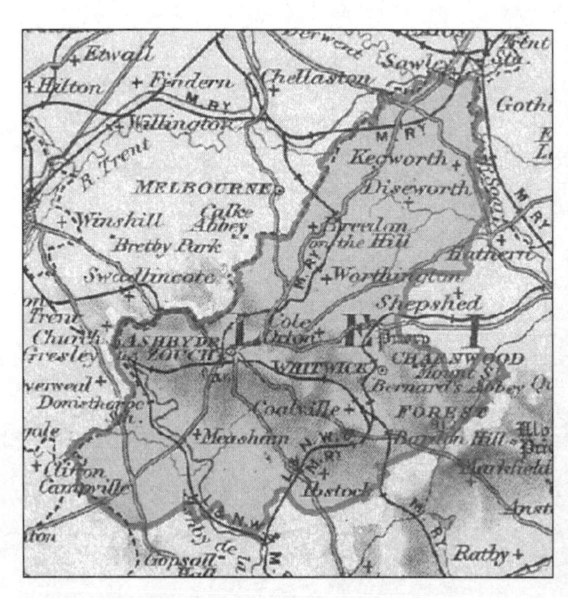

Area covered by the NW Leicestershire District Council

All that was swept away in 1974 when the rural district councils were exchanged for the mega district and borough councils. Charley came to rest then where it still does in 2009, under the careful oversight of the plainly named authority, the North West Leicestershire District Council, with headquarters at Coalville.

2 31st AUGUST 1940

A Special Birth

GEC telecommunications engineer Tom Ridley was in the middle of what would be a momentous day for him, and even more so for his wife, Isabelle. Early on in that year 1940, Isabelle confided in him the good news that in the summer, they would be expecting the birth of their first child. The day had come, and Isabelle's mother was installed at their family home on 100 Heath Road, Coventry. It was time for Tom to go across town, and fetch the designated midwife, who had been caring for Isabelle during her pregnancy. The portents on his trek became ominous, a visit from the Luftwaffe was on its way. The air raid warnings were sounding, and when Tom reached the home of the midwife, she declined to leave her house, through fear of what might fall from the skies.

In spite of Tom's distress and persistence, the midwife still refused to come, but did give him the name and address of another suitable person across the town. So Tom mounted his bike and cycled across to the Stoke area of town. By now the air raid was in full swing, and it was dangerous to be outside. The second midwife refused to come. In desperation, Tom made for the home of Isabelle's grandmother, Granny Eccles. The ARP Wardens urged Tom to get off the street, but Granny Eccles responded to the call to come to the aid of her granddaughter. After a long and difficult labour, Maureen Ridley entered the world, weighing in at ten pounds. Isabelle was exhausted but much relieved, and took a very long time to recover from the experience.

But their new status as a family had begun. The maternal parental team looked after Isabelle and Maureen while Tom returned to his work at GEC. But all was soon to change. Perhaps because of the air raid, and knowing that the industrial nature of Coventry might attract many more destructive air raids, GEC decided to relocate to the Bradford area. So, very soon after Maureen's birth, her parents moved her away to a house right on the fringe of Bradford. Beyond the garden gate lay much open country, and not far away was the famous Ilkley Moor. Maureen's earliest experiences of being outside would have been much influenced by the openness of the local landscape.

Maureen's brother John was born in March 1944. This time, Isabelle was in the safe and reassuring confines of Ilkley Hospital for the birth. Maureen recounts that one of her earliest memories is one of the parties that were held to celebrate the end of the war. She was in a sack race, and for some reason, broke into tears inside the sack. Probably, like many children in the war, her playhouse was the family's Anderson shelter, the structure of corrugated sheet iron, half buried in the ground, to which you retreated to avoid the shrapnel.

When it was all over, but not until 1947, did GEC move its factory and its staff back to Coventry. That was a grim time, for not only was 1947 in the grip of the fiercest winter in living memory, the old home at 100 Heath Road was no longer standing, having been erased from the earth in that crescendo of fire and high explosive that was the wartime blitz. The raid that had raged overhead at Maureen's birth in August 1940 was later regarded as a dress rehearsal for the massive blitz the Luftwaffe inflicted on Coventry on the 14th of November 1940. The Ridleys had to lay their heads where they could. Isabelle and the children sheltered under 'midwife' Granny Eccles roof in Stratford Street, while Dad lived with mum for a while.

----oo000oo----

A modern daytime version of the view to the Coventry skyline that Charlie Brooks describes

Over in Charley, and just off the Oaks Road, opposite High Tor Farm, is a little turning off to the West alongside a wooded area. The woods hold the remains of an interesting story. A story about the time in the 19th century when the monks at Mount St Bernard abbey ran a reformatory to rescue young boys who had fallen foul of the criminal law system in Liverpool and other crowded urban areas. Just past these woods with all their memories and off to the right is Hillside Bungalow. It was built before the war by Charlie Brooks. A sensitive man, Charlie could not sleep on one night in November 1940. There was a very bright moon, and Charlie went out into the field in front of his house, turned right through the hedge into the next field and went up to the rocks that were poking through the surface on the crest. Behind him down below lay the monastery, the outline of the buildings clearly reflected in the moonlight, calm and peaceful. Above his head, the distant drone of many aircraft.

Ahead of him the urban area of Coalville, and a view stretching away towards Leicestershire's neighbouring county, Warwickshire. Charlie thought at first that the Luftwaffe planes were on their way to bomb Derby. But before long, the huge red glow on the horizon over the crest, told him that Coventry was the target. At first he was probably mesmerised by what he was witnessing. The drone of the warplanes continued unabated, and the intense red glow from the target was awe-inspiring. The drama he was witnessing went on and on for hours. Slowly it dawned on Charlie the awfulness of what must be happening in Coventry. His mind began to see pictures of homes and buildings wrecked and ablaze. His imagination stretched further when he realised that many men, women and children were suffering greatly or were dying. He wept uncontrollably.

In 1981, the Maureen Ridley born in Coventry in the house now being flattened while Charlie watched in 1940, came to live in Charley at St Joseph's Cottage. Maureen, now married to John Havers, got to know Charlie Brooks. Charlie told her the story of that night, sitting on those rocks in the moonlight, watching the horror being inflicted on Coventry. He filled out the story, painting vivid word pictures of the scene. Maureen recounts it like this:

> He said that the sky in the distance was lit up time and time again by flashes of light and then the red glow of fire; the sound of German planes could be heard even where he stood as they circled and turned towards Coventry and the flashes from anti-aircraft weapons and search lights on the ground made the sky almost as light as day. The noise was muted and very distant and he wondered if he imagined the sound of aircraft. The searchlights continued across the whole of the area he could see but the red glow crept across the view until the entire sky on the horizon seemed as if it was burning.
>
> Charlie was even then very upset by this memory and I asked him how he had felt at the time. He replied that he had felt very helpless, knowing that homes and lives were being destroyed as he watched but he could not leave to go home to bed but remained there until the early hours of the morning. There was a great sense of guilt, he said, that his life could go on more or less as it had for years while others were bereft of home, mother or father, son or daughter.
>
> It was the night of November 14th, the night a city was *Coventrated*.

In November 1940, in another house in Charley, another little family drama was being played out each time the air raid warning siren sounded. Down in the crypt of the solid Victorian Vicarage at The Oaks Church, Vicar Alfred Holden and his family took shelter. They would have heard about the massive blitz on Coventry, and probably on a later night in their shelter, as other bombers passed by overhead, their two children whiled away the time adding some poignant graffiti to the walls of the crypt.

Two images of the wartime grafitti recently discovered in the cellars of the old Vicarage

They put up the date, '15 November 1940, Heavy Raid Over Coventry', the message said in memory of the huge event. The Vicar's son had added a previous message to the walls of that secure place. He inscribed the date that the shelter was first used; 25th June 1940, at 1.10pm. A third panel bears representations of the faces of the family.

The Vicar and his family would prove to be a bulwark of stability in Charley as it geared up to face the war and all it brought with it. We shall hear more of this family.

The Oaks Vicarage at the heart of the wartime Charley Community

3 TAKING UP ARMS

Called or Volunteered for Active Service

As the nation edged towards war in 1938 its regular armed services were staffed on a volunteer basis. In 1937 the British Army numbered about 200,000 men, a number known by the Government as woefully inadequate to fight a possible war against Germany. The Government accordingly introduced the Military Training Act in April 1939 to require men aged 20 and 21 to register for six month's military training. There was some protective call-up of older key people that were going to be needed for the training of those men.

The declaration of war on 3rd September 1939 saw a burst of volunteering, but Britain could still only muster about 875,000 men in its armed services. In October 1939 the Government announced a programme of conscription, starting with men aged between 20 and 23, who were allowed a choice between the three services. As the war progressed, the call-ups ran up the age range. From 1941 single women aged between 20 and 30 received a call-up into vacant jobs on farms and in factories.

A full list of those from the Charley area who took up arms in World War 2 is framed on the south wall of the nave in The Oaks Church. We reproduce the names in the table on a following page.

Fifty two people are named in the list. We have not been able to find any accessible records of their service or units, other than those of the three who lost their lives in the conflict. Two women appear in the list, which implies that they donned a uniform in one of the womens' branches of the services. They were all clearly identified at the time though, as the Charley residents found a ready outlet for their concern in innumerable fund-raising efforts for the servicemen's *Comforts Fund*. Regular reports in the weekly Loughborough Echo pick up this stream of activity. On the 24th May 1940 the paper reported as follows:

> Mr J H Woodward presided over a meeting of Oaks Service Men's Comforts Committee on Tuesday evening at the Jolly Farmers Inn. Messrs Briggs, Brown & Jarvis were appointed trustees of the fund. The names of Messrs Lovett, Crowson and Haywood were added to the list of local men serving with the forces. It was decided that an additional gift of five shillings should be forwarded to each of the local men with the forces, and the Vicar was asked to undertake this. Plans were submitted for a roll of service which, it is proposed, shall be erected in the Oaks Church.

The week before, the paper noted that "Amongst the congregation at the Oaks Church on Sunday morning was Harold Burton-a former parishioner-who has come home for a brief leave to Shepshed, after service in Norway. Another local soldier who has returned from Norway was Michael Farmer, of the Abbey Lodge." Michael lost a leg in the conflict.

The Norway expedition of 14th April 1940 was an attempt to bolster the Norwegian defence in the face of the German advance up the coast from Denmark. It did not work, and the force was pulled out after fourteen days. This setback was not the only hard lesson the British Army learnt in 1940 from encounters with the ferocious efficiency of the German forces. In its edition of 7th June 1940, the Echo ran a two-column headline:

Loughborough Soldier back from Dunkirk.
Exciting Adventures. Skipper steers boat with propellers.

Some 300,000+ soldiers were rescued from the Dunkirk retreat, coming home to a country soon to feel the weight of the aerial onslaught of the Luftwaffe from its new bases in France.

The Oaks in Charnwood
Men on Active Service

John	Martin	E Diana	Martin
Edward	Briers	Horace	Dandy
Harold	Burton †	Cecil A	Beagley
Michael	Farmer	Charles	Allen
Frank	Gibbins	Alfred	Dandy
Joseph	Harriman	Ernest	Mee
John	Harvey	C William	Hall
Dennis	Harvey	Gordon M	Holden †
William	Squires	Peter J	Everett
Dennis A	Haywood	Albert E	Mason
George	Briggs	F Monica	Holden
Eric S	Spencer	Leslie	Dandy
Albert	Stock	William	Peat
Austin	Cook	George	Clamp
Arthur D	Rowlinson	Arthur J	Cockayne
Robert	Knight	Wilfred	Berridge
Fred	Goodacre	Norman	Bramley
Harry	Crowson	Laurence	Bowler
Herbert	Foster	Norman F	Hall
C Herbert	Haywood	Ronald	Stacey
Richard N	Lovett †	Clifford	Cockayne
Albert	Simpson	Ernest	Stock
Kenneth	Walker		
Walter	Marvin		
Eric T	Bailey		
Sarah	Hannagan		
Walter H	Taylor		
Walter	Burton		
H Ezra	Haywood		
Kenneth W	Spencer		

The List of those on Active Service in the order as in the Oaks Church. Some women crept in among the men!

The service men who received items from the *Comforts Fund* clearly appreciated these contacts with 'home'. The Echo edition of 7th June 1940 ran this report: "At a meeting of the Oaks

Service Men's Comforts Committee on Tuesday evening at the Jolly Farmers Inn, Mr Wilfred Taylor presiding, it was announced that several letters of appreciation had been received from local men with the Forces, who had received the latest gifts from the committee." These gatherings at the Jolly Farmers Inn were obviously very convivial ways to help the troops. The Echo continues: "Mr F Sherriff kindly supplied a prize for an interesting darts competition, in aid of the fund, and the winners were Mr Moore and Mr Burton. The top score was 200 in six arrows, and the lowest was six in six arrows. The competition raised 9s. 3d. The coal which was presented by Mr T Allen in aid of the Fund was won by Mr E. Briers."

The need to show solidarity with the Charley servicemen through the Comforts Fund found its way into the cultural lives of the local population. The Echo of 12th of July 1940 reports on the red letter day amongst the tennis enthusiasts and friends at the Oaks. The "tennis club organised a successful gala, the object being to provide support for the Comforts Fund and the Wool Fund in connection with the ladies Comforts Knitting Party." Mr Malcolm Grimley won the men's singles trophy, and Miss Kathleen Grimley triumphed in the ladies singles. The Oaks Club challenged Copt Oak and came out top by 11 sets to five. After the match about 70 sat down to an excellent tea in the parish room, and later the festivities took the form of a dance, to music provided by a radiogram. Mr R.G. Holden was the master of ceremonies, and the spot competition was won by the vicar and his daughter, Miss Monica Holden. Miss E Bowler, Mrs Hall and Mrs Grimley served up the refreshments, and the whole event raised the splendid sum of £9 15s 6d for the Comforts Fund.

The Comforts Fund Committee kept its eye firmly on the ball, especially with the Vicar, the Revd A. C. Holden, as its secretary. On the 19th of July, the Echo reports on the Tuesday evening meeting at the Jolly Farmers Inn. A letter had been received from Cpl. Joseph Harriman, appreciative of the Comforts Fund gift. It was also announced that Albert Simpson and Herbert Foster had joined up since the last meeting. The meeting voted a further sum of five shillings to be distributed to the men on the list. On the 26th of July the Echo reported that Kenneth Walker and Walter Marvin were joining the forces bringing the total of men for the Oaks and Charley district to 24. On the 2nd August the Echo reported that the committee had changed its venue to the White Horse Inn for that Tuesday's meeting. Thankyou letters were read out from Arthur Rowlinson, Harry Crowson, Robert Knight, Fred Goodacre, as well as Messrs Walker and Simpson. It was further reported that the Service Roll had been constructed and that it would be consecrated the following Sunday in the Oaks Church. After remaining on display until the following Sunday, it would be placed in position on the wall.

The Roll itself had illuminated gold lettering with a scarlet border in knot design, and was framed in oak. At the dedication service, the Vicar preached on the text "His servants shall serve Him". The Echo went on to report that: "the Vicar spoke of Service as the watchword, and of the Forest home, from which these men had gone to their appointed posts of duty, as the heart of England, where in honest toil, generations had been schooled to prize and guard our great inheritance."

Come the autumn a further very large challenge was taken up enthusiastically and reported each week in the Echo. The great worth of the Spitfire aircraft was now very well-known by the population. All over the country funds were being set up to buy more Spitfires to replace those lost and to add to the squadrons. Shepshed and Oaks in Charnwood had its own Spitfire Fund and each week the Echo published the names and amounts of every donation. The list resembles the electoral roll of the locality, with seemingly every person represented. Later on the 29th of November the Echo reports on collections being made for the Coventry sufferers, reflecting the huge damage and injury inflicted by the massive Luftwaffe blitz earlier that month. The sum of £3 15s 6d was sent to the Mayor of Coventry. Miss Diana Martin of Charley Hall, joined up in December 1940, and her name was to be added to the Service Roll in the Oaks Church.

If you were a man, and either too young or too old to join the regular forces, then the chance to serve came with the formation of the LDV, the Local Defence Volunteers, or the Home Guard as this fighting defence force came to be known. Members of the Charley Heritage Group have been able to record conversations with some of those LDV members. Here are snippets from farmer Dennis Poole, born on 2nd February 1923, telling his story at 6 Bawdon Cottages, answering questions in 2008 about his wartime memories. His words are presented in his own delightful vernacular speech.

"Well I was at Charley Mill Farm at the time, and we had to join the LDV. We 'ad arm bands, and the arms were ball shot, and buck shot [fired from shotguns]. This was really illegal, if we had used it under the Geneva Conference, they would have split a man in half.

So we got a uniform, and then .303 rifles, couldn't fire them as they were. They'd been packed in grease and we 'ad to clean them, and learn how to use 'em. And we got 15 rounds, that's all we was allowed to carry.

Interviewer: Whereabouts were you based at the time?

Charley Park, part of Charley Hall. And we used to shoot into the bank at the back for practice.

Interviewer: Were you stationed down at Charley Hall then?

Well Anywheres. Privates' Pub they would call it. When we was all night on manoeuvres they would get in 18 gallons of beer. Alec Marston...he were Lieutenant. Lt Booth was boss of us.

There were a rifle competition for all the country. We had to hit a moving target and I was 80th over all the country in that. Had a letter from the King, one of the top hundred I was. We practiced on targets up against a bank. A bull's head was painted in the centre, and magpies away from the middle. Mr Parker used to tell us if we 'ad a bull or a magpie.

We used to have a bus to take us. But George Rees he were in Woodhouse Home Guard and he used to take his butcher's van and his pigeons and let 'em go. It was the only way he could do it cos he weren't allowed to use it any other time. The bus driver once took us down Green Hill. At the top of Green Hill there were sandbags where Coalville Home Guard used to sit, in case the Germans came up the hill from Coalville. Any road, we loaded up the sandbags on the bus and took 'em for ourselves.

Interviewer: What was it like down at the Hall in those times?

Johnny Martin was the boss then. I used to shoot foxes for 'im. We were on manoeuvres one night and I saw a fox right up on the skyline and I let my gun off at it. Everybody thought the Germans had come and went on full alert.

One air raid we 'ad I got down behind a wall and the bomb came down near the pit...the water hole. The bomb crater we then used to use for Mills Bomb practice. We used to draw a line across half way up, and throw the bombs and then duck down. It was a bit scary, cos one chap didn't draw the pin out and it never went off. We were bombing all morning round it trying to make it go off. We could hit it but it wouldn't go off because he hadn't pulled the pin out. When the Lieutenant bounced down the field he picked it up."

Dennis Poole would have been a member of the Charnwood Battalion's Forest Company, with its HQ at Maplehurst, just above Woodhouse Eaves. Austin Ruddy, in his monumental study of the Leicestershire Home Guard *To the Last Round*, Breedon Books, 2007, lists Lieutenant C.Z.M. Booth as being in charge of No.3 Platoon, HQ Ulverscroft. Dennis Poole says his HQ was at Charley Park, implying he was in No.4 Platoon, which Austin Ruddy lists Charley Hall's J. B. Martin as in charge.

Les Cooke also told his Home Guard story to a tape recorder as well. He was in the Loughborough Battalion's 'C' Company-Shepshed & Hathern. Its No. 12 Platoon was styled as the Blackbrook Platoon. Here are his recollections in 2004:

"My depot was at Reservoir House. We met there. I'll tell you what, we was on the dam one night and there were all these lights down at the bottom and of course, I was the youngest and they put me in some rhododendron bushes, one round of ammunition and they said “Anybody comes, you say Halt! Who goes there”. Any road they went and inspected these lights and they were glow-worms you know. But I've seen two Canadians in a Tiger Moth - two Tiger Moths and they were practicing bombing on the reservoir and one got in the reservoir and he got drowned and the other one managed to get down off the field.

Interviewer Maureen: Did you tell me before that he got drowned because he got caught in the weeds?

Yes, there was a lot of weeds round the reservoy [reservoir in the local vernacular]. There was a lot of willows on the edge of the reservoy and it’s so funny to say that was the edge of the reservoy, the plane came down here and instead of him swimming that road, he swam this road and we found him in these willows, drown-ded. And then we fished a boy out that had stolen a boat.... some boys had stolen a boat and one of them got drown-ded. And just round Gun Hill there was a Dakota crashed there and every time we plough that field up now we always plough something up at that place. And then there was another plane dropped , just the other side of the reservoy that we call Botany Bay and they dropped some bombs in the reservoy. They also dropped some bombs down Tickow Lane; they dropped some bombs at the back of the Fox at Thringstone...and they dropped 26 incendiary bombs in one of our fields.”

Photographs of the two Home Guard outfits appear overleaf.

There were a number of plane crashes on Charnwood. Heritage Group Member Michael Froggatt read up on the official stories of three. On the 8th March 1941 a Tiger Moth on a training flight from Desford crashed at Newtown Linford. On the 15th February 1943 a Wellington bomber crashed at Hermitage Farm near Whitwick and on the 17th September 1945 a Miles Martinet crashed at Brickhill Farm Woodhouse Eaves. The Wellington crash was recorded in the official daily Chronicle at Mount St

'C' Company (Shepshed and Hathern) 9th Loughborough Battalion of the Leicestershire Home Guard.
Commander J Nichol at the centre behind the big drum.
Page191, To the Last Round, Austin J Ruddy.

Colonel J B Martin is at the centre of this photograph.
The Colonel was in charge of No. 4 Platoon (Charley) of the Charnwood Battalion of the Home Guard.

Bernard Abbey for 15th February 1943, in these words: 'Late this afternoon, during a snow squall a huge Wellington Bomber crashed at Gun Hill, about half a mile away. The machine ran into some trees and turned over, killing the crew of four or five and scattering bombs round the adjoining fields. Fortunately the bombs did not explode but a huge sheet of flame went up from the burning petrol'.

Another contributor of eye witness testimony is Bill Stanley, OBE, who farmed at One Barrow Lodge for 34 years, and was a long standing Church Warden at The Oaks. He writes about another plane crash, and his experience in the Blackbrook Home Guard Platoon:

"On 18th November our daughter Enid Elizabeth was born in the Nursing Home, Radmoor Road, Loughborough. This was during the German air raids on Coventry, Derby and surrounding towns when I would cycle to the Nursing Home in the evenings. As there were no other men around, the matron was pleased for me to stay until the 'all clear' sounded. Enid was put in a clothes cupboard with a baby boy born at the same time until the all clear sounded.

The nearest we had was a stick of bombs dropped on Willie Bowley's farm at B lackbrook; it was thought that the railway line through Shepshed was mistaken for a main line. On another occasion an America fighter plane nose-dived into a field at Finney Springs when debris was scattered over a wide area. The pilot had been thrown out and all I could do was spray his headless and legless body, which was still burning, with a fire extinguisher. The wreckage was guarded by American Soldiers (G.I.s) whose main occupation was firing at pigeons and other birds with their rifles and giving souvenirs from the plane to anyone going near.

At about this time the Home Guard was formed and all of us on the farm joined the Shepshed Company. As a German invasion was threatened, I was in charge of a platoon guarding the dam at Blackbrook day and night based in a sand-bagged hut in the middle of the dam. The nearest we got to warfare was seeing flares and incendiary bombs being dropped on Derby. We were relieved at the weekend by men, who after a Saturday night out, were both a little beer happy and trigger happy. Our H.Q. was in the Board Room at the reservoir house with the reservoir keeper and his wife sleeping in the bedroom above. On one occasion a bullet went through the ceiling and passed through the bed in which they were sleeping!

As the threat of invasion subsided the ammunition was taken away from us. I did have an issue of lead balls for firing from a double-barrelled sporting gun but these were extremely dangerous to use because if the barrel was choked too much there was a danger of splitting the barrel of the gun."

Tom Hopkins of Whitwick also wrote his recollections of this plane crash and the arrival of the Americans to sort it out:

"This is what I can remember about the plane crash in the field near where I lived many years ago in One Barrow Lane, off Charley Road. I had been poorly for two days and my mother was in the bedroom cleaning the windows. I was sitting up in bed and we both heard this terrible noise and I rushed out of bed and looked up into the sky and saw an aeroplane on fire, just missing the top of the house. I think the pilot avoided the house even though he was doomed and then the plane blew up and most of the bits ended up in Mr. Stanley's mangold field. Well, for a few moments everywhere went quiet then all hell broke out.

My uncle was down the lane trying to start his car; bits of the plane were flying all round him and my mother rushed out of our house and into next door. Mrs Ethel Rose and my auntie on the end house all came into the yard. Well, she was the only one with a telephone so she rang the Police at Shepshed and they were soon up. Us kids were very excited as this was a new thing for us country bumpkins but the police would not let us near the field.

The next day the Yanks came as it was one of their planes. They turned up mid-afternoon and proceeded to try and put up tents but that day it was raining and everywhere was a sticky mess - mud everywhere. One of the head men came and knocked on my Mam's door and asked her if she would make them a hot drink. She said yes, but remember we were on rations and not much to go round, so a hot drink was made and then she said "How many of you?" "About 12 people" So we made room for them, some slept on the living room floor and some slept on furniture. Anyhow they all got a good night's sleep in the dry and warmth. Next morning when they left we followed them down to the field and they put up tents and barriers round the crash site. We sort of kept getting in the way but not a word was said to us. They had plenty of food, bananas and oranges, chewing gum and food we could not have had because of rationing. Getting back to the crash material... .one large chunk of metal was in my uncle's fowl pen right behind the house. Bits must have gone into the reservoir but the most bizarre object was the pilot's head still in his flying helmet which we found in a large bramble bush on the lane. His eyes were open. My uncle found one leg in his flying boot in among his cabbages.

It took a good many weeks to find most of the pieces and I think if the reservoir was ever cleaned out a lot more pieces would come to light. Even to this day when the field is ploughed pieces of the plane still keep coming up and lots of live ammo keeps coming to the surface. When the Yanks were satisfied, they cleaned up all the bits and then they removed their tents and when the last vehicle was leaving, they called at our house and left my Mam a tea-chest full to the brim with fruit, tea, coffee, sweets, chocolate and thanked her very much for giving them shelter the first night. A legacy they left was all alongside of the reservoir - they chopped the spruce trees down to keep their campfires going so the ones that are left are massive and small ones are still growing."

These sorts of event were the only real excitement experienced by the Home Guard, who maintained its alertness until D-Day in 1944. After that the formations all had their group photographs taken prior to standing down, their efforts no longer being needed.

Of the 52 names on the service roll in the Oaks Church, three are marked with a cross. They paid the ultimate price of victory. One was Harold, the 26 year old son of Albert and Lucy Burton, who lived on the side of Shepshed close to The Oaks. A private in the 7th Battalion, the Green Howards, he was flung into the fighting from D-Day onwards. His battalion was part of 30 Corps, fighting its way up the corridor from Eindhoven through towards Arnhem in the airborne-led operation 'Market Garden'. They made it as far as Nijmegen having then to fight hard to repel German counter-attacks determined to halt any further progress. Private Harold Burton fell in one of those fierce fights, and today his name is commemorated in the nearby commonwealth cemetery at Jonkerbos, on the edge of Nijmegen.

The War Cemetery at Jonkerbos, near Njimegen Holland

The Vicarage family of Alfred & Violet Holden were not immune from a similar tragedy of one of their sons. 22-yr old Gordon Michael Holden had joined the Royal Navy and had been trained as a Signalman. His ship, HM Trawler Rysa, was deployed in the Mediterranean in 1943 on minesweeping work at Maddalena, Sardinia, when it was itself destroyed by a mine. Gordon's grave is the sea, and his name is commemorated on the impressive Naval Memorial at Lowestoft, the original home of the first trawlers requisitioned by the Navy for war service.

The National Memorial to Naval Personnel lost at sea. Lowestoft

The third local man to be killed in action was the 25 yr-old Hussar, Trooper Richard Norman Lovett, also to die at sea. Part of the 4th Queen's Own Hussars, Royal Armoured Corps, Norman found himself in early 1941 being ordered out of North Africa into Greece. Hitler, having lost patience with the failure of the Italians to capture the Greek port of Piraeus, started to inject his own troops into Greece to take it himself. Piraeus was strategically vital to the German plans to sweep the allies out of Africa. The London Government decided that a special force of 50% British, 25% New Zealanders, and 25% Australians should be despatched to Greece from Africa to halt the German attack on Greece. For this book it was possible to interview Gordon Lovett, Norman's younger brother, at his home in Shepshed, who served as a Bomber Navigator in the Royal Air Force from 1942-47. Gordon offered the view that this commonwealth force was regarded as a *sacrifice force*, the Government knowing that it could not be properly supported and equipped in the time scale needed.

Gordon Lovett, who told this story of his Brother Norman

Trooper Norman Lovett in tropical kit in his desertised tank was plunged into the conflict in the winter conditions of the Greek mountains. The German blitzkrieg was overwhelming, and the decision was taken to evacuate as many troops as possible who were not already captured by the Germans. Chaotic conditions existed in the evacuation port and beach area of Naplion as boats took on troops to escape the turmoil. Two Royal Navy destroyers arrived offshore from Gibraltar, HMS Diamond and HMS Wryneck. Together they gathered up some 950 men from the chaos, but were sitting targets for the attentions of waves of Junkers Ju 87 dive bombers, the so called Stukas. Both were sent to the bottom of the Mediterranean with almost all hands. Only 23 men survived.

Trooper Norman Lovett had been on board the Wryneck, and since his grave is the sea, his name is commemorated on the Athens Memorial, set amid the beautifully kept grounds of the Commonwealth Cemetery of the capital city Norman strove to serve. He was awarded a special medal by the Greeks, reproduced on the following page.

Norman was the eldest of three brothers, all born in the front room at 18 Hawcliff Road, Mountsorrel. Middle brother Eric volunteered for the Royal Air Force, spending much of the war in Coastal Command. Gordon, known as Dick, was the Bomber Navigator of the picture above, and the teller of this story. Before he joined up, Norman Lovett was an Insurance Agent for the Prudential. Married in early 1940 to Rothley girl Lorene Frith, their family home was on The Oaks side of Shepshed, near to the deLisle Arms Inn. The widowed Lorene returned to live in Woodgate, Rothley , while her younger sister Betty Frith, who had married Ivan Betts, eventually went off to Australia after Ivan also became a war casualty. Mercifully, no more of those 52 names on the Service Roll in The Oaks Church were killed in action, living to enjoy the Forest again in freedom.

The immaculate Athens Memorial

The Greek Medal awarded to Norman Lovett

This scroll commemorates

Trooper R. N. Lovett
4th Queen's Own Hussars

held in honour as one who
served King and Country in
the world war of 1939-1945
and gave his life to save
mankind from tyranny. May
his sacrifice help to bring
the peace and freedom for
which he died.

Trooper Lovett's Medal Citation

4 DIGGING FOR VICTORY

Charley Farming Put To The Test

Embossed seal of the Ministry of Agriculture & Fisheries from the Charley papers at the PRO Kew. MAF 32/379/135

Even though in the run up to war the British Government had been dragging its feet on the pace of re-armament, in 1938 it began to revive a structure of County War Agriculture Executive Committees. Although organised by county, bringing together local people who knew their area well, the operation was firmly based at national level in the Ministry of Agriculture and Fisheries, the 'MAFF'. It was plain that Britain might soon be under siege, cut off from its free trade links to worldwide food exporters. Only a nationally co-ordinated system, it was felt, could maximise home food production, and yield the vital data to underpin decisions about rationing.

In the adjacent figure there is an early listing of the members of the Leicestershire 'War Ag', as the committees became known. This document was issued by MAFF and bears its embossed imprint and the date 1 September 1939.

1

DEFENCE OF THE REALM

ORDER OF APPOINTMENT OF WAR AGRICULTURAL EXECUTIVE COMMITTEE

COUNTY OF LEICESTER

In pursuance of Regulations 49, 51, 53, 62, 63, 66 and 85 of the Defence Regulations, 1939, the Minister of Agriculture and Fisheries (hereinafter referred to as "the Minister") hereby makes the following Order:-

The Minister hereby appoints the following persons to be the War Agricultural Executive Committee for the Administrative County of Leicester, for the purpose of doing such things as they may be authorised to do and exercising such powers as may be delegated to them under any of the said Regulations by Order of the Minister:-

J.T. Jacques, Esq., The Motts, Ibstock.
J.F. Montagu, Esq., Cold Overton Hall, Oakham.
W. Glover, Esq., Snarestone, Burton-on-Trent.
A. Crawford, Esq., Lowesby Hall Farm, Lowesby.
P.F. Astill, Esq., Cossington, Leicester.
J.R. Lambley, Esq., J.P., Hereward, Fairmount Drive, Loughborough.
Mrs. Munro, J.P., The Homestead, Thrussington.

The Minister further appoints J.T. Jacques, Esq., to be the Chairman and F.V. Millington, Esq., County Offices, Grey Friars, Leicester to be the Executive Officer of the Committee.

This Order may at any time be amended or revoked by any subsequent Order made by the Minister.

IN WITNESS whereof the Official Seal of the Minister of Agriculture and Fisheries is hereunto affixed this *first* day of *September* nineteen hundred and thirty-nine.

Donald Ferguson

The County Committee as at 1st Sep 1939

The make up of the County committee shifted from time to time. A significant addition took place when Charnwood farmer Howard Coltman was appointed in July 1940.

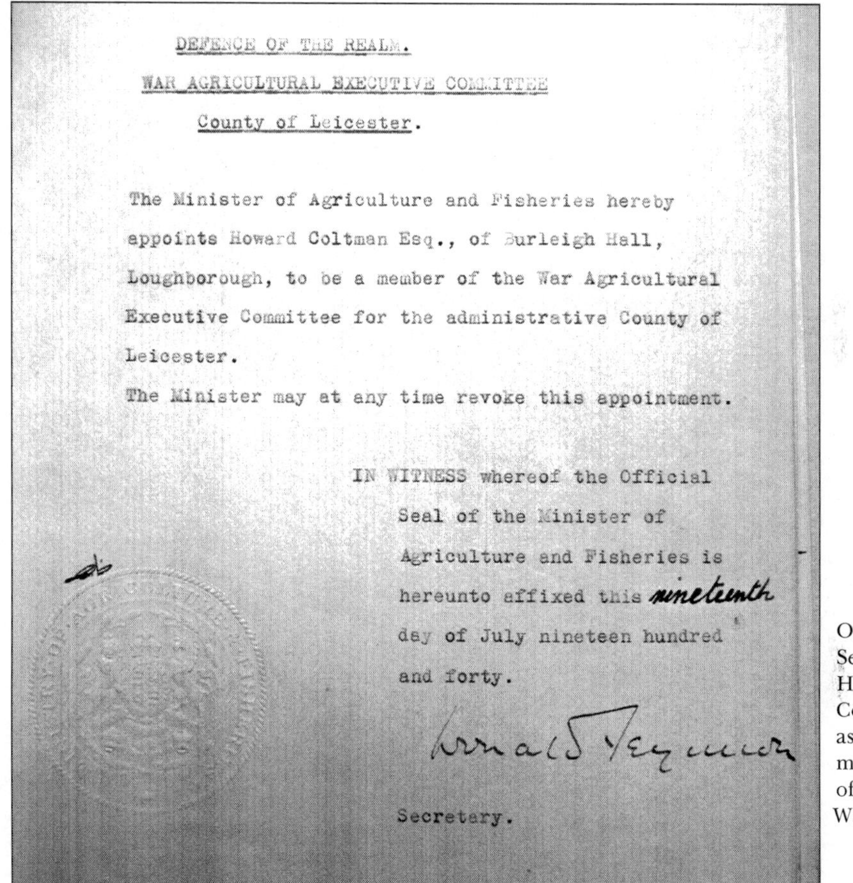
DEFENCE OF THE REALM.

WAR AGRICULTURAL EXECUTIVE COMMITTEE

County of Leicester.

The Minister of Agriculture and Fisheries hereby appoints Howard Coltman Esq., of Burleigh Hall, Loughborough, to be a member of the War Agricultural Executive Committee for the administrative County of Leicester.

The Minister may at any time revoke this appointment.

IN WITNESS whereof the Official Seal of the Minister of Agriculture and Fisheries is hereunto affixed this nineteenth day of July nineteen hundred and forty.

Donald Fergusson

Secretary.

Official Seal on Howard Coltman as member of County WarAg.

Mr. Coltman would know Charnwood well, based just over the border at Burleigh Hall, Loughborough. He sat alongside Lady Martin of The Brand, at Woodhouse Eaves, another close neighbour. The Committee lived up to the *Executive* in its title, meeting every Friday at 11am in the County Rooms in Leicester, spawning District-based sub committees, and a host of task-oriented sub groups. Charley came under the delegated authority of the Loughborough District 'War Ag', and from a listing preserved in the archives at the Public Record Office, here in the figure over the page are the members.

County ........LEICESTERSHIRE........

PARTICULARS OF DISTRICT SUB-COMMITTEES

District ........LOUGHBOROUGH........

How defined ....PETTY SESSIONAL DIVISIONS........
(R.D.C. or other boundaries)

Chairman ....H. COLTMAN, ESQ., BURLEIGH HALL, LOUGHBOROUGH.

Members ....W. H. BRICKWOOD, MANOR FARM, COTES, LOUGHBOROUGH

H. GORE-BROWNE, BROOMBRIGGS, WOODHOUSE EAVES,
NR. LOUGHBOROUGH.

W. H. MARSH, BURTON BANDALLS, LOUGHBOROUGH.

A. F. STANILAND, MANOR FARM, LONG WHATTON, LOUGHBOROUGH.

H. A. SWAIN, WHATTON FIELDS, LONG WHATTON, LOUGHBOROUGH.

E. E. WELLS, THE MOORS, KEGWORTH, DERBY.

C. Boucher, 117. Nottingham Road, Leicester.

The Loughboro Committee

Anyone who held or occupied land deemed capable of being part of the food chain was conscripted into this comprehensive system under the terms of the Defence of the Realm Act of 1939. The Minister for Agriculture was given very wide powers to control and direct food production, even to the extent of removing inefficient farmers from their tenancies or holdings. A massive drive was launched to plough up at least ten per cent of existing grass pasture, and to plant food grains instead. The pill was sweetened with a government grant of £2 per new acre ploughed, backed up by constant pressure from officials from the War Ags.

The ploughing campaign threw up many difficulties from among the farmers. Some pleaded that they had no knowledge of arable farming, while others did not have access to the necessary equipment. The County Committees spawned an array of specialist sub-committees to source and deploy equipment, knowhow and materials in the battle to increase output and efficiency on their farms. Leicestershire had nine such sub-committees, Coltman and Lady Martin featured on several in the list.

Typical posters of the period, urging the farming fraternity to believe in its value.

By April 1940 the national target of two million acres of newly ploughed land had almost been reached. Leicestershire had been doing its bit, as the Loughborough Echo reported in its issue of June 7th, 1940. This regular farming column set out the County War Ag's stated aim of 25,000 acres of grassland in the county to be under the plough for the 1940 season. The report was happy to state that up to 18th May 1940 the Committee had served ploughing-up orders for 28,923 acres of grassland for the 1940 harvest. The Committee had also dealt with 1,785 acres of grassland which it had ordered to be fallowed for the 1941 harvest, 206 acres to be re-seeded to grass, and 466 acres of existing arable land on which it had served cultivation orders. This made a total of 30,914 acres of grass to be ploughed and 466 acres of arable. The Echo went on to report that the Committee had carefully estimated that of this acreage 29.958 acres had actually been ploughed, some of the difference being accounted for in the use of ordnance acreage which includes field features such as ponds, ditches and headlands. The Loughborough District Sub-Com-

mittee had substantially completed its programme of inspection, and by 18th May had certified 23,068 acres as eligible for the Ministry Grant of £2 per ploughed-up acre.

Charley figured in the ploughing-up campaign. A study of the rear page of the 1941 Survey forms shows the Inspector's rendering of the fields and acreage ploughed up for the 1940 harvest and the type of crop grown. In most cases it was Wheat or Oats.

Here is a listing of the acreage ploughed up in Charley allowing for a crop harvest in 1940:

No	Farmer	Farm	Acres
1	W Blackett	Vale	28
8	P Macer	Bess Bagley	4
14	B Renshaw	The Oaks	12
16	The Abbott	Mt. St. Bernard	12
17	F Woodward	Greenhill Lodge	15
18	F Woodward	Rock	14
19	Sherrif	Chitterman Hills	63
21	G Wooliscroft	One Barrow	7
22	W Blackett	Charley Knoll	10
25	J Smith	Billa Barra	6
		Total Acres	171

In the summer season that followed there were labour shortages, and the farmers increasingly came to value the worth of the burgeoning force of girls in the Women's Land Army. Nationally, by May 1940, some 6,000 Land Girls were deployed, and during that summer harvest camps of school children became a new feature of life in the countryside. Farmers were squeezed both ways for labour, as the conscription of young men for the armed forces began to bite, and the amount of work increased from the newly ploughed acres. At every meeting of the Loughborough District Sub-Committee of the War Ags, petitions were lodged for delay or deferment of call-up of essential farm workers. The District Committee had the power to issue deferment certificates, especially when allowing the call-up would mean the serious depletion of the capacity of its farms.

Labour tensions emerged in 1940. Why would a young man work on a farm for 35 shillings a week (£1.75) when he could earn £6 a week working for a contractor on military construction projects? In July 1940 the government instituted a statutory minimum weekly wage of £4.85. Parallel adjustment had to be made to the guaranteed price regime for foodstuffs to enable farmers to meet commitments and to yield enough of a surplus to allow for investment in further efficiency improvements.

That the Loughborough Echo would elect to publish a piece from *The Farmer and Stock-Breeder* on the Boiling of Pigswill showed just how innovative pig producers had to be. The War Agricultural Committees were progressively given additional resources to assist them with their work. Expert professional advisers were at the call of the various committees and could be drafted in wherever their help was needed. The minutes of the Loughborough District Sub-committee have many references to farmers having to deal with colonies of rabbits enjoying access to their crops. An expert in dealing with such pests was retained and the minutes recall many occasions when he was dispatched to deal with these rogue colonies. Oakley Wood was a particular haunt of these furry creatures.

The Committees had contractors who could move in on to land and carry out substantial drainage improvements. Such use of machinery became vital in the continuing drive to raise the efficiency of farm operations. With the emphasis across British industry of manufacturing material and equipment for the fighting war, the supply of tractors and implements for farms was most reliant on lend-lease supplies making their way across the Atlantic on the convoys from America. Local War Ags knew very well which of their farmers could most benefit from new equipment, and the minutes record many instances of Charley farmers taking delivery when such equipment became available.

The 1941 Farm Survey records that there were 55,000 tractors across the country, but by the spring of 1945 the number had risen to over 200,000. Combine harvesters were unheard of in 1941, but by 1945 there were 2400 such pieces of equipment in use.

The *For the Farmer* column in the Loughborough Echo of 19th July 1940 ran a news item that showed how the harvest could be affected by a problem unique to wartime. *Heavy Penalties for Sightseers Damaging Farm Crops* ran the headline. A new £50 fine had been introduced for damaging crops by trespassing on agricultural land. In a recent incident negligible damage had been done by a bomb in a wheatfield, but the entire wheat crop on 25 acres had been ruined by being trampled on by sightseers.

The harvests of 1941 and 1942 were each much bigger than in previous years. In 1943, the national target of 600,000 extra wheat acres was realised, but it took the conscription of women into the Land Army and the extensive use of labour from among prisoners of war to keep productivity up on the farms. In 1943, land girls worked 50 hours a week in summer and 48 in winter. Their pay rose to 22s 6d per week (£1.125), board and lodging being provided by the farmer. The peak complement of land girls was 87,000 during the year 1943. Progressively, prisoners of war took on the task of farm labour. Nationally, in 1941, 2400 Italians were engaged in helping with the harvest. In 1942 some prisoners were even living out of camp, directly on farms, and by July 1943, there were 37,000 prisoners of war at work on farms across the country. 1943 was the peak year for food production, but even though the weather did not help farming efforts through 1944, by the end of the war agriculture was in a wholly different and better state unimagined in the dark days of 1938/9.

The Cooke family of Drybrook Farm tell of a remarkable event in a field called Cabbage Hill close to the reservoir. The field had been planted with the fodder crop known as the cow cabbage with the object of harvesting it when partly grown for selling on to other farmers to grow on. The harvesting task was very labour intensive, requiring each plant being pulled from the ground, bundled into 20s, and tied with raffia. The farmer was fortunate in having access to a squad of 100 prisoners of war from the camp at Garendon. They put their backs into it and the story goes that a world record one million plants were harvested in that operation.

Little groups of prisoners of war were deployed at Mount St Bernard Abbey to help with nonstandard tasks. An elderly Brother Gabriel, speaking in the Abbey shop in 2005, remembers one such group which was working in Tin Meadow on a drainage project. The experience left him frustrated for all the conversation and banter heard among the Germans was in their own language, which Brother Gabriel could not understand. This rare opportunity the normally silent Cistercian had to hear people talking was spoilt by not being able to understand the language.

One of the members of the Charley Heritage Group in 2009, Joyce Burton, was a wartime baby growing up at Low Woods Farm, Belton, just to the north of the Charley boundary. Whilst her childhood memories of farming practices relate really to the end of the war and the year or two afterwards, they vividly illustrate how things were done at that time. Joyce relates:

"**Potato Picking** usually took place in October, around the time of half term holiday. I don't know which came first, potato picking, or the holiday. A lot depended on the soil conditions; if the soil was damp the potatoes were spun out with clods of earth sticking to them. It was backbreaking work, collecting the potatoes in buckets, then carrying them to sacks, which were placed strategically along each row. The family turned out to help with as many willing children as possible. I also remember ex-prisoners of war who remained in the area. Pay was by the day, plus the largest potato you could find for your dinner the next day!

The job of **Muck Spreading** started in the summer months after the animals had been put out to grass. With the sheds empty the winter's supply of muck was dug out of the sheds. This was really hard work for those who tackled this job with a fork. The bedding was really matted together and trampled well down. It was taken out to the fields and spread by being thrown out from the back of a trailer.

The muck from the cow sheds was cleaned out twice a day, usually after milking, and stacked in the middle of the yard, cleared away once a year. There was a very nice smell in the cowshed during winter, always warm, the sweet smell of hay and cow poo, contentment!

There was great excitement when the **Threshing Machine** came along, with extra help in tow. Gran always fed the workers at lunchtime with 'bag puddings', which were suet puddings made with a mixture of meat, onion, jam and fruit, cooked in a large cloth, and secured with string and a safety pin. It was usually Mr Barker of Bunkers Hill Farm, Shepshed, who came with his machines. On one occasion, the engine kicked back and the starting handle hit him in the face. The men carried him into the farmhouse. There was blood everywhere, and Mr Barker was out cold. I thought he was dead! All my cousins were around with 'thacking pegs' and dogs, ready to catch the rats and mice as they were disturbed by the men on the stack as they threw the sheaves into the machine. The chaff (husks from the grain), was saved for bedding for chickens. There was always screaming, shouting, dogs barking and sticks flailing! Great fun by all.

Children were sent indoors when it was the time for **Killing the Pig**. Then the pig would squeal, the deed would be done, and the dead pig would be taken over to the dairy, where the blood was caught and the body dealt with. Never allowed to see this! Gran would have the fire ready and banked high, with kettles on the boil. We as children, couldn't wait to get the bladder to play with, but only on grass as it was rather delicate. Aunts would be around the scrubtop table, each with a job to do. This was a time of abundance, the smell fantastic, with black puddings, faggots, brawn and everybody's favourite pork scratching, especially in sandwiches with salt!

The large pork joints were hung for several days, before being prepared for salting. The halves of a pig, leg or shoulders, were placed in a slate sink usually six feet long and three feet wide, large enough to take a side of bacon. Blocks of saltpetre were cut up and rubbed into the carcass, a process that took place over several days, to encourage the liquid out of the meat. This done, the joints would be hung up to drain before being taken into the house, and hung on a hook from a beam for final drying in the alcove by the fire. A curtain was placed across the alcove so that the body could not be seen by visitors!

Often **storage clamps for potatoes** were made in the same field from which the potatoes were picked. Care had to be taken to find a dry area, which was preferably close to the farm. Food was in short supply, and clamps were quite often tampered with during the night. Potatoes were placed on a straw bed in a long mound with height and length varied to suit the crop. Battens of straw were placed on the top with soil above that, all patted down with the back of a shovel. If a frost free shed was available, potatoes were stored indoors. Small or damaged potatoes were boiled in the copper in the washhouse outside in the garden and fed to the pigs. The smell of these was great on a cold day.

Carrots were also clamped, but not so many carrots were grown around here, as they usually grew best in a light sandy soil. Dad grew a sizeable amount for our family use. He grew beetroot in the same way. **Brussels Sprouts** were often harvested as complete 'legs' in links and hung up in the cool shade. What comes around goes around, it now being fashionable again to buy the vegetable this way".

The whole 'regiment' of wartime farmers in Charley numbered 25. They were very closely monitored and supervised by the war agricultural executive committees. Addressograph plates for each farm were held in the War Ag Office at 7 Friar Lane, Leicester. In the spring and early summer of 1941, the Ministry conducted the National Farm Survey. This was like a modern Domesday Book of agriculture across the country. Each holding was identified by a unique number, and the names and addresses of both the owners of the land, as well as the occupiers,

A Summary of the data on the 24 Farms within the Charley Parish No. 135

Sourced from the Charley papers at the PRO Kew MAF 32/379/135

1941 Farm Table									
MAF No. 135/	Farm Name	Parish	OS Map	LOB	MAF Grade	Farmer	Owner	Acres	Years On
1	Vale Farm	Charley	24NW	209	A	William Blackett	Williams, Chitterman	246	12
2	Charnwood Heath	Charley	24NW			Ernest Burton		3	20
3	Moult Hill Orchard	Charley	24NW			James Bowler		3.5	21
4	Charnwood Lodge	Charley	24NW-27SW	56	A	SW, TC, CE Clarke	SW & CE Clarke	217	30
6	Charley Hall	Charley Hall	24NW	448	B-	John B Martin	John B Martin	37.5	14
7	Kirkham Gardens	Charley Hall	24NW			John B Martin	John B Martin	28	20
8	Bess Bagley	Ulverscroft	24NW	456	B	F A Macer	S Livingstone	57.5	5
12	Charley Mill	Charley	24NW	449	B-	William Poole	Clarke/Williams/Herrick	222.5	5
11	Birch Hill	Copt Oak	24NW	449	B-	William Poole	Clarke/Williams/Herrick	do	5
13	High Tor	Charley	24NW-27SW	402	B-	William Revell	SW & CE Clarke	132	6
14	Oaks Farm	Charley	27SW	289	A	Mrs B Renshaw/AT Wright	SW & CE Clarke	138	6
15	Hill Farm	Charley	24NW	584	B	GW & CR Siddons	Williams	66	8
16	MSB Abbey	Charley	27SW	232	A	Father Superior	MSB	188	103
17	Greenhill Lodge	Charley	24NW	231	C-	FH Woodward	SW & CE Clarke	187	14
18	Rock Farm	Charley	24NW-27SW	157	A	JR Woodward	John B Martin	157	6
19	Chitterman Hills	Ulverscroft	24 All	213	A	CH & FC Sherriff	Livingstone/Jones/Elliott	303	1
20	Dry Brook	Charley	27SW	233	B+	Stanley Walker	EMP deLisle	85	4
21	One Barrow Lodge	Charley	27SW	234	A-	George Wooliscroft	EMP deLisle	150	4
22	Charley Knoll	Charley	27SW	498	A-	M A Blackett	C Sherriff	182	40
23	Bawdon Cottage	Woodhouse	24NE	443	C	A E Barker	(also at Burleigh Farm)	54	22
24	Whittle Hill	Woodhouse	27SE	284	C	George Poole	Curzon Herrick Estate	112	21
25	Billa Barra	Charley	24NW	624	B	J C Smith	J H Williams	11.4	3
26	Burleigh Farm	Nanpantan	27SE	397		L Barker jnr	(also at Bawdon Cottage)	63	10
27	Oaks Cottage	Charley	27SW	258	B	John Renshaw	P Paget	45	4
28	Poultney Cottage	Ulverscroft	24NW	204	C	Charles Webb	S Livingstone	57	7
							Total Acres	2745.4	

were set out As well as returns covering the type and acreage of crops, labour, motive power and other details, each farm was inspected and graded on a three-point scale. Farms graded A were judged as efficient and the farmers as competent. Farms graded C, were at the other end of the scale, and before long, drastic changes had to take place on these holdings. Unless the action resulted in very substantial improvements in efficiency and output, the holding was more than likely put into the hands of a competent farmer. Much attention was given by the War Ags to Farms graded B to enable them to improve.

All the documents resulting from this survey are kept at the National Archives at Kew. At the same time, ordnance survey maps at the 6 inch scale from the 1920s or early 1930s were annotated in colour to show the precise layout and extent of each farm holding featuring in the survey. The table on the previous page summarises the 2,745 acres of Charley which became the engine of the parish's principal contribution to the war effort. Eight of the holdings were given an 'A' grade, with four falling into the 'C' category. Much as would be expected in any set of data. Some outstanding performers at the top, some almost failures at the bottom, and a range of middling outcomes in the body of the data.

On the following pages a representative sample set of the farm survey returns for just one of the farms are set out, to show how it was done. The farm featured is the small Drybrook worked by Stanley Walker on land owned by Edwin de Lisle, which now in 2009 is the farming base for Heritage Group members Roger and Sandra Cooke. A summary page for each farm can be found at the close of the book in Appendix A.

MR.STANLEY WALKER, LR/192
DRY BROOK FARM, 135/20
COALVILLE,
LEICS.
95/9

135/20

20

FARM SURVEY

9 acres Rough Grazing.
84½ Total acreage.

County Leicester. Code No.
District Loughborough. Parish Charley.
Name of holding Drybrook Farm. Name of farmer S. Walker.
Address of farmer as above, Coalville, Nr. Leicester.
Number and edition of 6-inch Ordnance Survey Sheet containing farmstead 1922 Ed. XVII SW

A. TENURE.

1. Is occupier tenant ... X
owner ...
2. If tenant, name and address of owner :—
S.Mr. de Lisle, Esq.,
Garendon Hall,
Loughborough.
3. Is farmer full time farmer ...
part time farmer ... X
spare time farmer ...
hobby farmer ...
other type ...
Other occupation, if any :—
Producer- Retailer.
4. Does farmer occupy other land ? Yes / No: X

Name of Holding	County	Parish

5. Has farmer grazing rights over land not occupied by him ? ... Yes / No: X
If so, nature of such rights—

B. CONDITIONS OF FARM.

1. Proportion (%) of area on which soil is

Heavy	Medium	Light	Peaty
		100	

2. Is farm conveniently laid out ? Yes ... / Moderately X / No ...

	Good	Fair	Bad
3. Proportion (%) of farm which is naturally		80	20
4. Situation in regard to road		X	
5. Situation in regard to railway	X		
6. Condition of farmhouse		X	
Condition of buildings		X	
7. Condition of farm roads		X	
8. Condition of fences	X		
9. Condition of ditches	X		
10. General condition of field drainage	X		
11. Condition of cottages	None.		

	No.
12. Number of cottages within farm area	–
Number of cottages elsewhere	–
13. Number of cottages let on service tenancy	–

14. Is there infestation with :—	Yes	No
rabbits and moles		X
rats and mice		X
rooks and wood pigeons		X
other birds		X
insect pests		X
15. Is there heavy infestation with weeds ?		X

If so, kinds of weeds :—

16. Are there derelict fields ? Yes / No: X
If so, acreage ...

C. WATER AND ELECTRICITY.

Water supply :—	Pipe	Well	Roof	Stream	None
1. To farmhouse		X			
2. To farm buildings				X	
3. To fields	X			X	

	Yes	No
4. Is there a seasonal shortage of water ?		X
Electricity supply :—		
5. Public light		X
Public power		X
Private light		X
Private power		X
6. Is it used for household purposes ?		X
Is it used for farm purposes ?		X

D. MANAGEMENT.

1. Is farm classified as A, B or C ? ... B+
2. Reasons for B or C :—
old age ...
lack of capital ... X
personal failings ...

If personal failings, details :—
Not quite an "A" Farmer, but tries very hard.

	Good	Fair	Poor	Bad
3. Condition of arable land		X		
4. Condition of pasture		X		

5. Use of fertilisers on :—	Adequate	To some extent	Not at all
arable land		X	
grass land		X	

Field information recorded by
R.T. Payne.
Date of recording 16.4.42.

This primary record completed by

Date ...

Form No. B496/E.I.

*14940. Wt.46166/817. 8000 pads. 3/41. Wy.L.P. Gp.676.

The Inspector's report on farm No. 20 on the Charley list. Mr Walker is given a B+ grade with a typical school report type comment: *Not quite an 'A' Farmer, but tries very hard.*

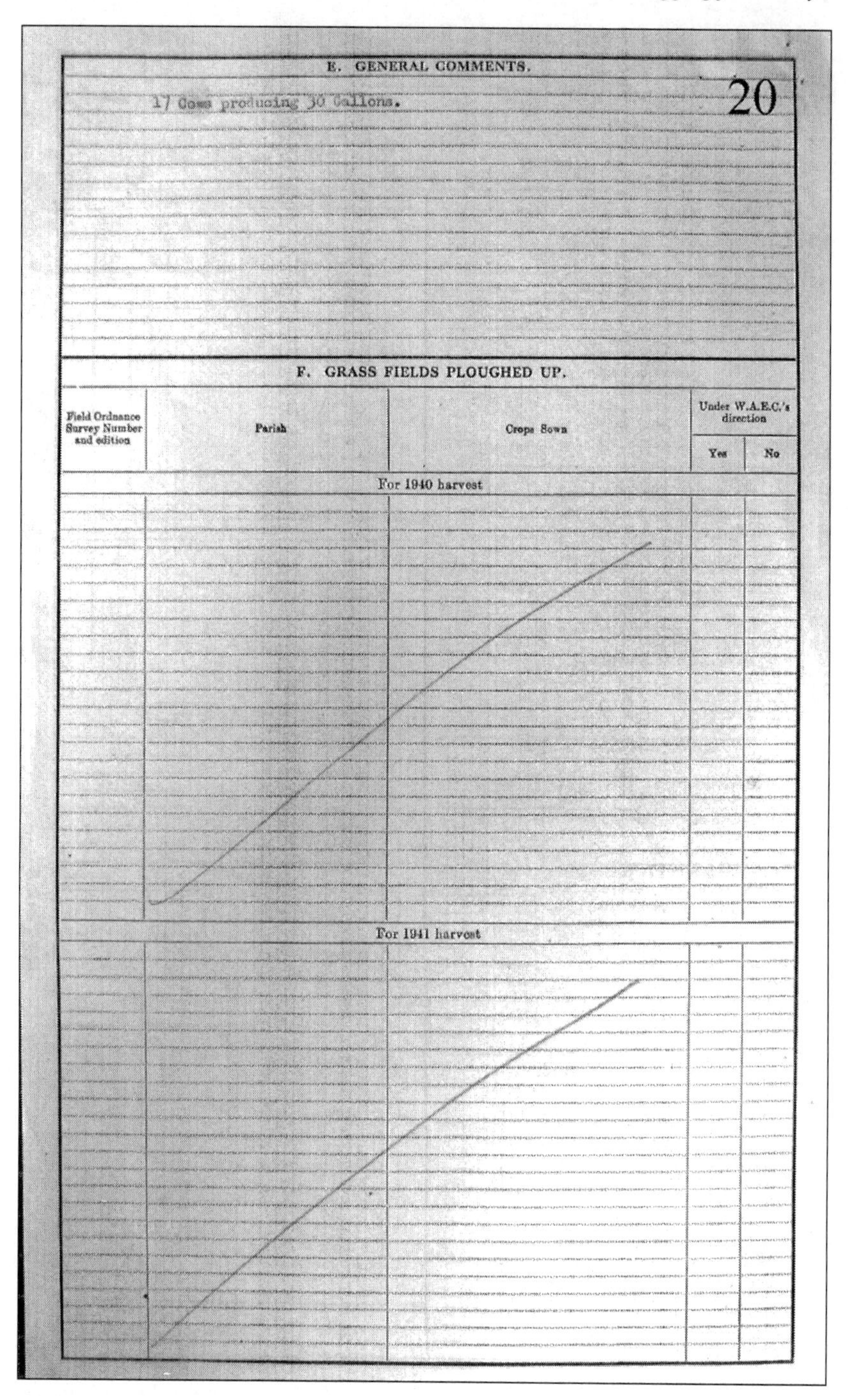

E. GENERAL COMMENTS.

20

17 Cows producing 30 Gallons.

F. GRASS FIELDS PLOUGHED UP.

Field Ordnance Survey Number and edition	Parish	Crops Sown	Under W.A.E.C.'s direction	
			Yes	No
For 1940 harvest				
For 1941 harvest				

Side 2 of the Inspector's Survey Report. No scope for ploughing up previously grass fields. Just one comment on this side: *17 cows producing 30 gallons.*

File in both Forms 3MISS. (Green) and C.47/S.S.Y. (Blue)

MINISTRY OF AGRICULTURE AND FISHERIES.

THE DEFENCE REGULATIONS, 1939, AND THE AGRICULTURAL RETURNS ORDER, 1939.

RETURN WITH RESPECT TO AGRICULTURAL LAND ON 4th JUNE, 1941.

	CROPS AND GRASS	Statute Acres
1	Wheat	6
2	Barley	
3	Oats	4½
4	Mixed Corn with Wheat in mixture	
5	Mixed Corn without Wheat in mixture	6½
6	Rye	
7	Beans, winter or spring, for stock feeding	
8	Peas, for stock feeding, not for human consumption	
9	Potatoes, first earlies	
10	Potatoes, main crop and second earlies	½
11	Turnips and Swedes, for fodder	2
12	Mangolds	5
13	Sugar Beet	
14	Kale, for fodder	1
15	Rape (or Cole)	
16	Cabbage, Savoys, and Kohl Rabi, for fodder	
17	Vetches or Tares	
18	Lucerne	
19	Mustard, for seed	
20	Mustard, for fodder or ploughing in	
21	Flax, for fibre or linseed	
22	Hops, Statute Acres, not Hop Acres	
23	Orchards, with crops, fallow, or grass below the trees	
24	Orchards, with small fruit below the trees	
25	Small Fruit, not under orchard trees	
26	Vegetables for human consumption (excluding Potatoes), Flowers and Crops under Glass	
27	All Other Crops not specified elsewhere on this return or grown on patches of less than ¼ acre	
28	Bare Fallow	
29	Clover, Sainfoin, and Temporary Grasses for Mowing this season	2
30	Clover, Sainfoin, and Temporary Grasses for Grazing (not for Mowing this season)	
31	Permanent Grass for Mowing this season	20½
32	Permanent Grass for Grazing (not for Mowing this season), but excluding rough grazings	24
33	TOTAL OF ABOVE ITEMS, 1 to 32 (Total acreage of Crops and Grass, excluding Rough Grazings)	76
34	Rough Grazings—Mountain, Heath, Moor, or Down Land, or other rough land used for grazing on which the occupier has the sole grazing rights	9

LABOUR actually employed on holding on **4th June.** The occupier, his wife, or domestic servants should not be entered.

			Number (in figures)
35	WHOLETIME REGULAR WORKERS — If none, write "None"	Males, 21 years old and over	
36		Males, 18 to 21 years old	2
37		Males, under 18 years old	
38		Women and Girls	
39	CASUAL (SEASONAL or PART-TIME) WORKERS	Males, 21 years old and over	
40		Males, under 21 years old	
41		Women and Girls	
42		TOTAL WORKERS	2

	LIVE STOCK on holding on 4th June, including any sent for sale on that or previous day		Number (in figures)
43	Cows and Heifers in milk		13
44	Cows in Calf, but not in milk		4
45	Heifers in Calf, with first Calf		
46	Bulls being used for service		1
47	Bulls (including Bull Calves) being reared for service		
48	OTHER CATTLE	2 years old and above — Male	
49		2 years old and above — Female	
50		1 year old and under 2 — Male	
51		1 year old and under 2 — Female	4
52		Under 1 year old:— (a) For rearing (excluding Bull Calves being reared for service)	3
53		(b) Intended for slaughter as Calves	
54		TOTAL CATTLE and CALVES	25
55	Steers and Heifers over 1 year old being fattened for slaughter before 30th November, 1941		
56	SHEEP OVER 1 YEAR OLD	Ewes kept for further breeding (excluding two-tooth Ewes)	
57		Rams kept for service	
58		Two-tooth Ewes (Shearling Ewes or Gimmers) to be put to the ram in 1941	
59		Other Sheep over 1 year old	
60	SHEEP UNDER 1 YEAR OLD	Ewe Lambs to be put to the ram in 1941	
61		Ram Lambs for service in 1941	
62		Other Sheep and Lambs under 1 year old	
63		TOTAL SHEEP and LAMBS	NONE
64	Sows in Pig		
65	Gilts in Pig		
66	Other Sows kept for breeding		
67	Barren Sows for fattening		
68	Boars being used for service		
69	ALL OTHER PIGS (not entered above)	Over 5 months old	
70		2—5 months	
71		Under 2 months	
72		TOTAL PIGS	NONE
73	POULTRY — If none, write "None"	Fowls over 6 months old	30
74		Fowls under 6 months old	
75		Ducks of all ages	
76		Geese of all ages	
77		Turkeys over 6 months old	
78		Turkeys under 6 months old	
79		TOTAL POULTRY	30
80	GOATS OF ALL AGES		NONE

	HORSES on holding on 4th June		Number (in figures)
81	Horses used for Agricultural Purposes (including Mares kept for breeding) or by Market Gardeners	(a) mares	1
82		(b) geldings	4
83	Unbroken Horses of 1 year old and above	(a) mares	
84		(b) geldings	
85	Light Horses under 1 year old		
86	Heavy Horses under 1 year old		
87	Stallions being used for service in 1941		
88	All Other Horses (not entered above)		
89	TOTAL HORSES		5

Form No. C.47/S.S.Y. 20 M-14000 5/41 (S2-4851)

N Walker

Mr Walker's Crops Return, signed off by him at the bottom. Trying hard to operate a mixed operation around his milk production.

S.F.

MINISTRY OF AGRICULTURE AND FISHERIES

AGRICULTURAL RETURN, 4th JUNE, 1941.

20

LABOUR ON 4th JUNE (Supplementary Questions).

			Number
	Of the **REGULAR** workers returned on page 1 (Questions 73—76) how many are:—		
129	WHOLE TIME FAMILY WORKERS {father, mother, son, daughter, brother, sister of occupier or his wife, but **not** other relations}	male	1
130		female	
	Of the **CASUAL** workers returned on page 1 (Questions 77—79) how many are:—		
131	EMPLOYED ON THE HOLDING THROUGHOUT THE YEAR BUT FOR ONLY PART OF THEIR TIME	male	
132		female	

MOTIVE POWER ON HOLDING ON 4th JUNE.

	FIXED OR PORTABLE ENGINES (Excluding Motor Tractors)	Number in figures	Horse Power of each
133	Water Wheels or Turbines in present use		
134	Water Wheels **not** in use, but easily repairable		
135	Steam Engines		
136	Gas Engines		
137	Oil or Petrol Engines		
138	Electric Motors		
139	Others (state kinds)		

NONE

	TRACTORS	Number in figures	Horse Power of each	Make or Model of Tractor
140	Wheel Tractors for field work			
141	Wheel Tractors for stationary work only			
142	Track laying Tractors			

NONE

NOTE.—Subject to the special Question No. 134 engines or tractors that have been discarded or worn out should not be included.

RENT

ANNUAL RENT PAYABLE FOR THE HOLDING TO WHICH THIS RETURN RELATES.

		£
143	State the actual rent payable during the current year (*i.e.*, the contract rent **less** any abatements but **including** any interest payable on improvements)	
144	If the holding is **owned** by you, give the best estimate you can of the annual rental value	71

		Acres	£
145	If the holding is partly owned and partly rented by you, state:— Acreage of land which you own and its estimated rental value		
146	and Acreage of land which you hold as tenant and the rent payable (for definition of rent see Question No. 143)		

LENGTH OF OCCUPATION OF HOLDING.

		Years
147	How many years have you been the occupier of the holding to which this Return relates?	4
	or	
148	If you have occupied parts of the holding for different periods, give length of occupation for each	Part 1..........acres..........years Part 2..........acres..........years Part 3..........acres..........years

FOR OFFICIAL USE ONLY.

Mr Walker has no motive power of any sort at Drybrook. Just 5 horses.

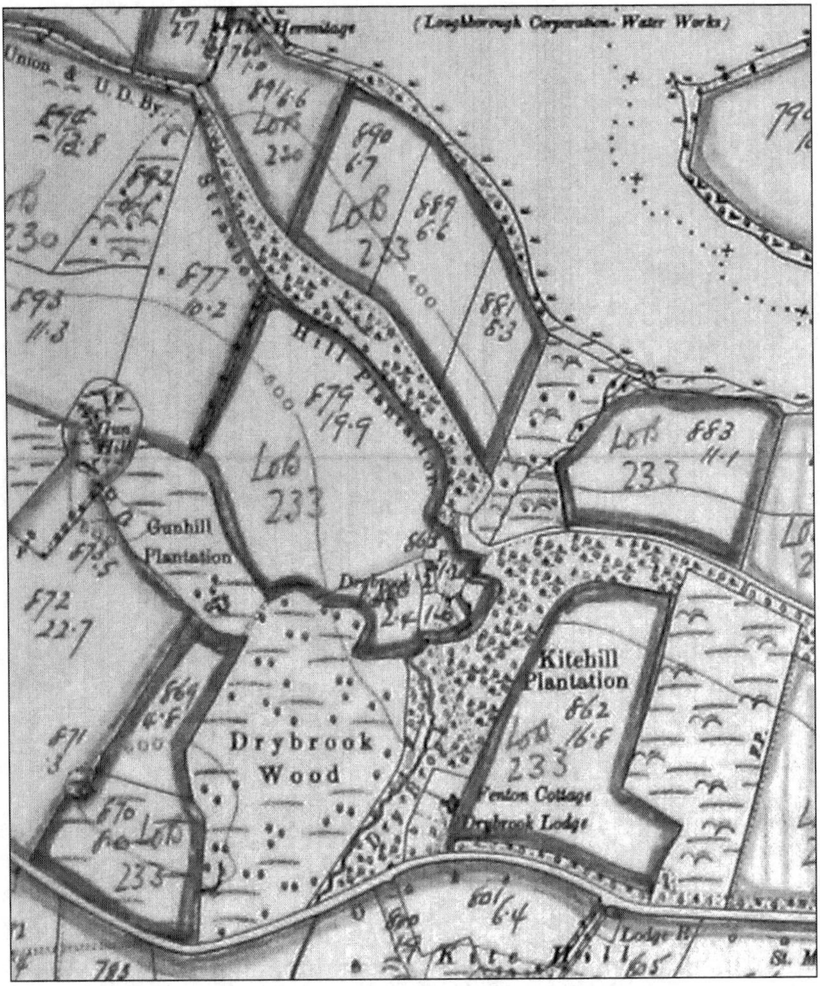

The Drybrook holdings are identified with the code **LOB 233** written into the spaces enclosed by the dark lines. The other numbers are the OS Field identifiers with the field acreages. Inset from map record MAF 73/22/24NW at the Public Record Office.

5 FOOD ON THE TABLE

Rationing, Nutrition and Inventive Catering

In 2009 we are used to an immensely abundant access to food not just as the raw materials for transforming into nutritious and tasty meals. Then we are absolutely spoilt for choice in being able to pick up all variety of ready prepared dishes from the chiller or freezer cabinets of our food shops, to simply heat up at home. Should that be thought of as too much bother, every kind of take-away outlet is but a short journey or a telephone call away. To cap it all, we can choose from a multitude of eating-out experiences, where we pay quite modest sums for someone else to put delicious food on an attractive table in front of us.

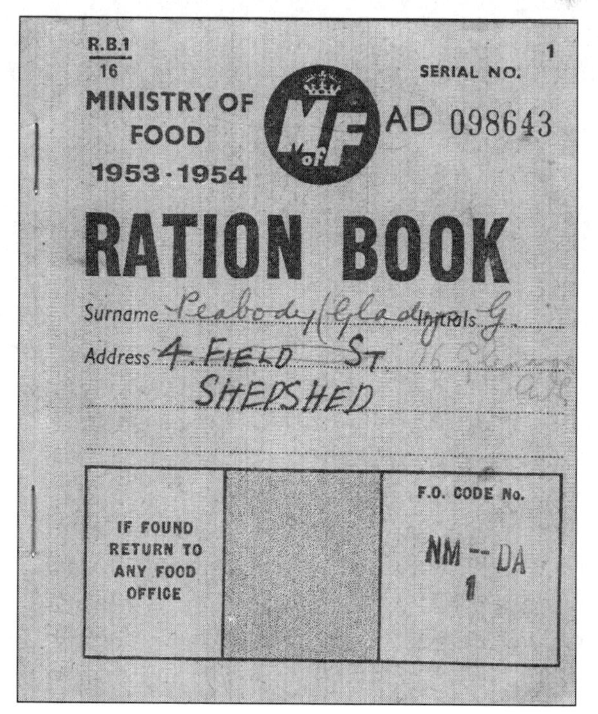

R.B.1
16
1
MINISTRY OF FOOD
1953-1954
SERIAL NO.
AD 098643
RATION BOOK
Surname Peabody (Gladys Initials G.
Address 4. FIELD ST
SHEPSHED
F.O. CODE No.
IF FOUND RETURN TO ANY FOOD OFFICE
NM -- DA
1

Mrs Peabody's Ration Book Cover 1953/4

The Charley Heritage Collection

Not so in the war years and for a decade afterwards in Charley and across the country. Take a look at the illustration here of the Ration Book of Gladys Peabody for the year 1953-54. Gladys lived at No. 4 The Lant, in Shepshed. She had to nominate which shop she would use for her ration of various foodstuffs. For meat, fats, cheese, bacon, sugar and no doubt, tea, she was a loyal fan of the Coop in Shepshed. But for eggs, Mr J Knight of The Lant was her supplier. With no shops in Charley itself, the residents had to lodge their coupons at shops off the Forest, like the Coop in Shepshed.

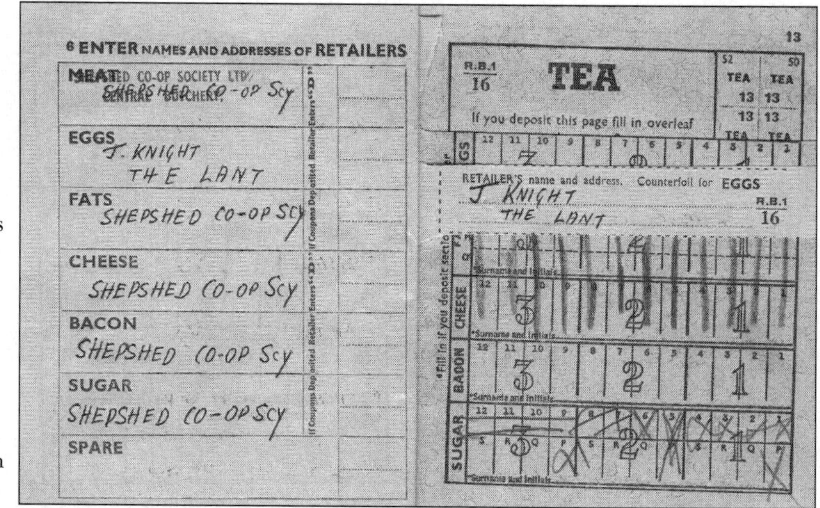
6 ENTER NAMES AND ADDRESSES OF RETAILERS

MEAT SHEPSHED CO-OP SCY

EGGS J. KNIGHT THE LANT

FATS SHEPSHED CO-OP SCY

CHEESE SHEPSHED CO-OP SCY

BACON SHEPSHED CO-OP SCY

SUGAR SHEPSHED CO-OP SCY

SPARE

13

R.B.1 16 TEA

If you deposit this page fill in overleaf

RETAILER'S name and address. Counterfoil for EGGS

J KNIGHT THE LANT

R.B.1 16

CHEESE

BACON

SUGAR

Mrs Peabody's Ration Book Inner 1953/4

The Charley Heritage Collection

Heritage Group member Michael Froggatt reviews the whole business of food rationing like this:

"Food rationing was introduced in late 1939 and petrol was in short supply and only available for essential journeys, but in March 1942 the basic petrol ration for civilians was abolished so any travel had to be on foot or bicycle causing cycles to be in short supply. Everyone was issued with a ration book. The basic food ration was obtained using coupons out of the ration book when presented to your supplier. In November 1939 people were ordered to register with shops of their choice i.e. a butcher, grocer, dairy. Ration books had to be handed in at hotels or billets but not needed in restaurants. If your shop of choice was bombed you had to register with another one. From January 8th 1940 the basic ration per person per week was:-

> 1lb or 1/10d worth of meat, offal not included
> 2 oz tea
> 2 oz margarine
> 2 oz butter
> 2 oz cooking fat
> 2 oz suet.

By March 1941 also included were jam, syrup, marmalade, honey and lemon curd at between 8 oz and 2 lb per month. In July cheese was rationed to 1 oz and eggs, milk and fruit varied with the seasons; thus the basic food ration varied during the war according to supply and production, the range was 1 shilling to 2 shillings and 2 pence worth of meat, 4 to 8 ozs bacon, 1 to 8 ozs cheese, 1 to 8 ozs fat, ½ to 2 eggs a week, ½ to 2 pints of milk, 2 to 4 ozs of tea and 8 to 16 ozs sugar (increased during the jam making season) Sweets and chocolate fluctuated at 3-4 ozs while soap became a serious problem at 4 ozs per month. One tin of National Dried Milk (four pints) was permitted every four weeks and every eight weeks the bonus of an extra twelve eggs was allowed in the form of the famous dried egg packet.

Movement in towns was easier because there was usually a regular bus service but on the other hand in the bigger towns and cities vegetables were often in short supply as not many homes had a big enough garden in which to grow their own vegetables; queues would form outside the greengrocers' shops and often after waiting an hour they would run out leaving half the people without anything.

National Dried Milk, the staple ingredient in every home

Milk became scarce because many dairy herds were slaughtered to release more land for vital food crops and as milkmen were directed away to fight it was more often delivered by a milk-woman driving the horse and cart on its rounds to fill the house-holders' jug when milk bottles were no longer made. In December 1941 cheap or free fruit juice and cod liver oil was made available to children under two years old but extended a year later to pregnant women and children up to the age of five."

The burden of serving satisfying food to the family table in each household fell in most cases on the woman, the housewife. In the Loughborough Echo of 12 April 1940 there was a story that spread across three columns under the headline 'MINISTER OF FOOD APPEALS TO WOMEN'. Subsidiary headlines were THE "KITCHEN FRONT", NEW IDEAS IN COOKING, Avoid Waste. The Minister of Food, Lord Woolton, is quoted as saying that "I hope the men will help, by encouraging the women, and not laughing at them. Kitchen food eaten fresh from the pan and the dish is just about the tastiest food anyone ever gets." Lord Woolton went on to say "that the country had had so much to choose from, that people had grown a little careless of food. Now they must take care of it and he gave these words of advice to the small consumer:

"If you each waste a slice of bread a day, it needs 30 shiploads of wheat a year to make up the wastage. Please take care with sugar, we are consuming more than we ought. In wartime then it should be one spoonful of tea for each person, and none for the pot. It is our patriotic duty to use potatoes properly." In another column in the Echo Lord Woolton described our food as our defence. He urged that everybody must take thought about our food and plan our buying and our cooking wisely. He described this as the "direct contribution to the national war effort

Another Govt. Poster urging careful use of food.

which people can make in their own homes. No other service is as close to our hands. To one and all of us the opportunity comes every day."

The Echo ran a regular weekly feature 'Recipe of the Week'. It reflected the reality of rationing and dealt with what was likely to be available. On the 6th of January 1940 the recipe was for Roast Rabbit. Rabbits were said to be foremost in butchers' displays at that time. That same week, the bacon ration was fixed at 4 ounces per person per week. In the issue of 19th of January 1940, the Echo offered Cow Heel Soup as its recipe for the week. On the 7th of June 1940 Braised Lamb featured as the recipe. The article suggested that about 3 lbs of scrag end of neck of lamb makes a delicious dish when cooked in this way. Sliced onion, a little salt and several peppercorns, went into the mix at the beginning, plus later some finely sliced cabbage or spring greens. Thickened later with gravy powder if available.

Just as the farmers were urged to plough up meadow land to grow wheat, so the population was continually exhorted to dig for victory in their gardens and in their allotments. It became a necessity for many as a means of adding to the sparse diet that rationing brought in.

Every possible technique of persuasion was used to inspire people to grow their own food

With Charley being a country place, and many people being involved in farming, access to additional food was easier than for townspeople. Joyce Burton, who in the previous chapter described life on a farm just after the war, adds these recollections about garnering the food from gardens and the rabbit warrens:

"Bottling kidney beans. Dad was a very keen gardener, producing beans 22 inches long! The beans were sliced very fine, and then placed in layers of saltpetre and excess liquid allowed to drain off. They were covered with greaseproof paper, and patiently tied with string. These were horrid and a waste of time and effort.

Bottling fruit. A really memorable smell of autumn. Plums, blackberries and gooseberries. Out came the Kilner jars to be sterilised and rubber rings, purchased usually from Randall's, the travelling Ironmonger and Hardware man, who called every Monday afternoon, bringing the paraffin delivery.

Winemaking. You name it, my mum could turn it into wine! Mum and Dad had quite a lot of visitors, and Dad was dispatched with the jug to get the wine from the 'Grey Hen', a 5 gallon ceramic barrel with a tap.

Nettle beer was always made in the spring, and said to be full of vitamins. The nettles were boiled, then filtered and sugar added, before allowing to cool. Toasted bread was floated on, liquid yeast on top. After fermentation came the bottling process. My memory is that it was always best to open Nettle Beer bottles outdoors as disasters were frequent.

Rearing poultry. Dad always ordered day old chicks from Carlisle. They would be put on the train early morning and delivered to Shepshed Station, or latterly, to Loughborough by teatime. The brooders were taken down and dusted, chaff put down and lamps lit on the day of arrival. Remember these chicks had not drunk or eaten, and still had their egg teeth. These were grown on until Christmas when they would be killed, plucked and gutted-all blood and feathers for about a week. At home, no wonder mum was tired and really didn't enjoy Christmas, but it was a way to make a living.

Long Netting of Rabbits was always done at night. Several people were needed with ferrets and dogs. Long nets 3 to 4 feet high and 100 yards long, and made of hemp, were used. The rabbits were bolted out of their burrows by the ferrets and dogs straight into the net, where they were dispatched by the catchers. Another method of catching rabbits was to put a small purse net over each hole in the set, and use the ferret to bolt the rabbits into each net. Ferreting is best done in the daylight. Modern technology has made ferreting easier by way of putting a collar on the ferret, with a transmitter. A ferret that has killed and fed on a rabbit may not surface for a couple of days. The ferret eventually has to be dug out.

Jugged Hare. The process means catching and saving as much blood as possible. Onions are fried with thyme and sage, the joints are browned, and then the blood and elderberry wine added. After a long slow cook in a casserole dish in a Rayburn, it makes a lovely meal served with mashed potato and root vegetables. Roast pigeon is another harvest to be collected or stored. Just the breasts of the birds are used, unless the need for meat is desperate! An excellent basis for a stir fry."

A few years ago Sheila Bass sat down with The Oaks Senior Citizens and came up with a bundle of recipes used in wartime to fill the tums of the families. The recipe titles give a flavour of

Faggots

8oz streaky bacon, minced
8oz pork belly, minced
8oz pigs liver, minced
4oz breadcrumbs
2-3 medium onions, chopped
salt & pepper
good pinch of dry mustard
6oz stewed apple
1 large egg, well beaten
2 good pinches of chopped parsley
2oz suet

Mix the meats and suet. Add breadcrumbs, onions, salt and pepper, mustard and parsley. Add the apple pulp and egg. Mix well and shape into balls, place on a baking dish. Bake for 45 minutes in a fairly hot oven.

Sheila Bass
Oaks Senior Citizens

The Oaks Senior Citizens memory of a wartime recipe for Faggots.

their recollections. *Misers Feast*, based on a piece of bacon with lots of vegetables, baked. *Miners Fruit Cake*, made from dried fruit when available with 8 oz of dripping to stick it all together. *Cottager's Pie*, where the meat from a boiling fowl is stripped into a frying pan and browned with the usual flavourings, carrots and onions, then baked in an oven under a covering of sliced potatoes. *Hunters Stew* saw all the eatable bits of pigeons, rabbits and a bit of bacon served under a pie crust. Apart from the *Faggotts* recipe featured in the panel, perhaps the most intriguing offering from Sheila Bass's collection was the *Oggyot*. This was an alcoholic egg flip said to be given to nursing mothers *to thicken their blood*! Often otherwise taken by anybody as a hot nightcap, it was a mixture of half a pint of milk laced with two eggs, two tablespoons of rum, and a tablespoon of sugar. That would keep anybody going through a night in the air raid shelter, or sentry duty at the Reservoir Gatehouse Home Guard Post.

An *Oggyot* a day keeps the blues at bay.

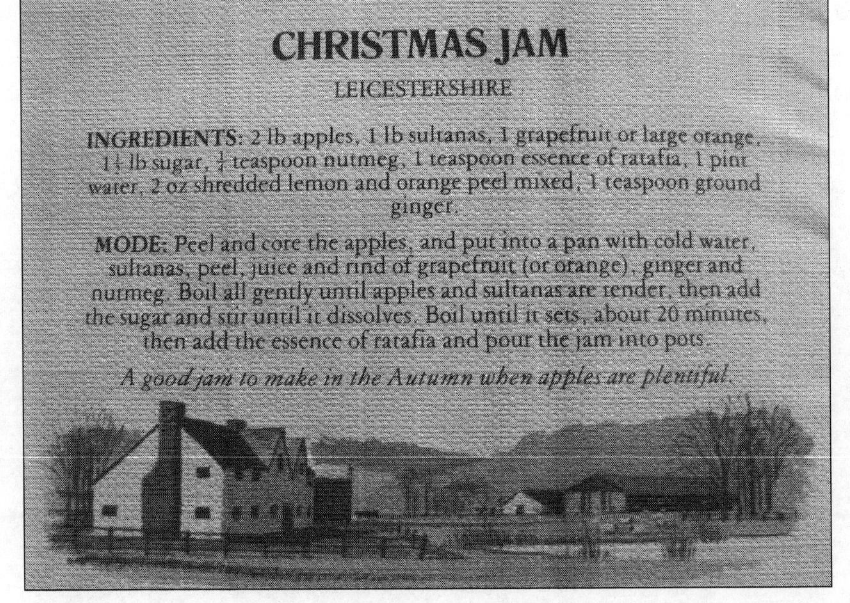

CHRISTMAS JAM

LEICESTERSHIRE

INGREDIENTS: 2 lb apples, 1 lb sultanas, 1 grapefruit or large orange, 1½ lb sugar, ¼ teaspoon nutmeg, 1 teaspoon essence of ratafia, 1 pint water, 2 oz shredded lemon and orange peel mixed, 1 teaspoon ground ginger.

MODE: Peel and core the apples, and put into a pan with cold water, sultanas, peel, juice and rind of grapefruit (or orange), ginger and nutmeg. Boil all gently until apples and sultanas are tender, then add the sugar and stir until it dissolves. Boil until it sets, about 20 minutes, then add the essence of ratafia and pour the jam into pots.

A good jam to make in the Autumn when apples are plentiful.

For when the items were available

From a book of the time

6 LIFE & VISITORS

The Stories of People

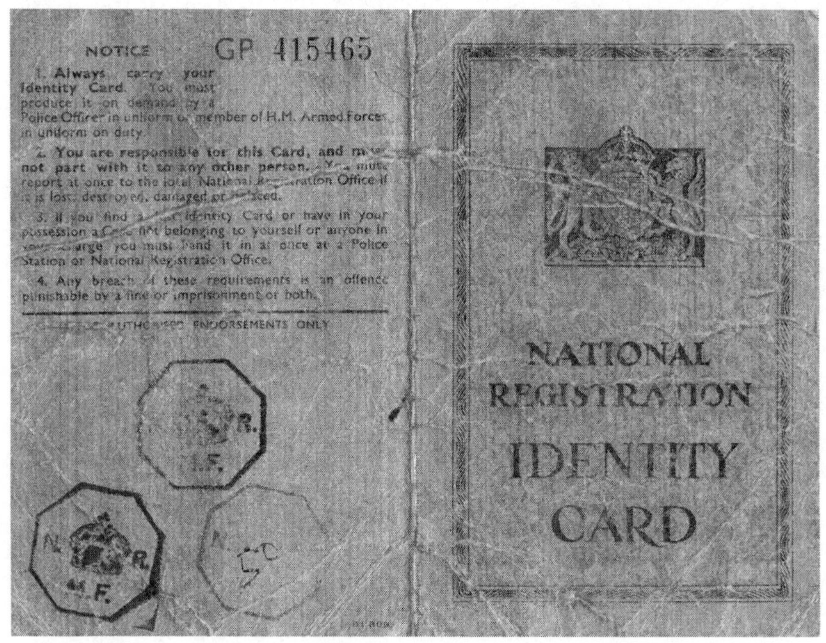

NOTICE GP 415465

1. Always carry your Identity Card. You must produce it on demand by a Police Officer in uniform or member of H.M. Armed Forces in uniform on duty.

2. You are responsible for this Card, and must not part with it to any other person. You must report at once to the local National Registration Office if it is lost, destroyed, damaged or defaced.

3. If you find a lost Identity Card or have in your possession a Card not belonging to yourself or anyone in your charge you must hand it in at once at a Police Station or National Registration Office.

4. Any breach of these requirements is an offence punishable by a fine or imprisonment or both.

AUTHORISED ENDORSEMENTS ONLY

NATIONAL REGISTRATION IDENTITY CARD

A well used example of the card carried by everyone

What was ordinary life like for Charley people during World War Two? Rationing and the preoccupation with getting enough food to the table have already been examined. The heavy weight of expectation and government supervision bearing down on the farmers has filled an earlier chapter. The anxiety among many families for the safety of their sons in the armed forces would always have been in the background. Getting about became more difficult as the supply of petrol for incidental journeys by car dried up.

Nobody of course could go anywhere without their National Identity Card. Avoiding 'Careless Talk Costing Lives' became a new habit for everyone. The older men were often absent from the home fireside doing their duty in the Home Guard platoons. But coming together at local events did not stop, and as has already been seen, many of them were given an added purpose as fund-raisers for worthy causes like the Hospital Fund, or the Comforts Fund for the serving soldiers.

A charming example of the Govt. Poster campaign to remind the people of a present danger

Robert Holden, son of the Vicar at The Oaks Church, worked hard in the Scouting movement as Assistant District Commissioner. Each Palm Sunday at The Oaks a church parade was staged, and as The Echo reported on 22nd March 1940, that year's parade was attended by Scouts from Snibston, Hugglescote, Thringstone, Loughborough, Oadby, Whitwick, and the Oaks. Wolf Cubs came from The Oaks, and Girl Guides from Coalville, Whitwick, and Loughborough. This impressive turnout was inspected by T M Walters, District Commissioner.

The presence in Charley of a resident Vicar and his family at the Oaks Vicarage throughout the war gave a focus of unity for many in the parish. Vicar Alfred Holden promoted an annual summer beanfeast as a way of bringing together all the church groups. The Echo of 19th July 1940 reported that the gathering in the Parish Room of the Communicant's Guild, the Bellringers, the Parochial Church Council, and the Sunday School Scholars and Teachers "did ample justice to an elegant repast, and activities were subsequently transferred to the Vicarage Lawn." "Later a move was made to the grounds of Charnwood Lodge, by kind permission of Mr S W Clarke". The Oaks had a tradition of holding services in the open air on some summer Sundays.

The one at the beginning of August 1940 was held on Mr A Peberdy's field on the Ashby Road. The Oaks choir led the singing, and the parade was preceeded by the Red, White and Blue Band, under Mr B C Gibbins. The Echo of 19th July 1940 reported that a congregation of 500 straddled the summit of Iveshead for the annual event there.

Vicar Alfred Holden was of course there for the special times in the lives of local families. In August 1940 Mary Ann Burton, wife of his verger & sexton Ernest Burton, of Charnwood Heath, died after a long struggle with illness aged just 55. In September 1940 the last surviving member of the Thompson farming family, Miss Annie Grace Thompson died in her 70th year. Her father had farmed at The Oaks until his death, a tradition that was carried on by his widow and then his sons and Annie. Annie was living quietly nearby at St Mary's in retirement when she died. Alfred Holden was a good friend to both families at this time, and officiated at the burials in the churchyard with calmness and dignity.

Heritage Group member Michael Froggatt is a keen observer of Forest affairs. His family eventually farmed at Charley Knoll, and in retirement, and from that vantage point, he guards the south eastern corner of Charley Parish. He has some interesting viewpoints on life in wartime:

"Anyone under the age of sixty might be very surprised to learn of the things that were set up in our area as little evidence of them is still visible, but with some research and observation certain things can still be found.

If permission is granted for a field walk in one of the fields on the left of Charley Road travelling in an easterly direction, there can be found the raised plinths of the searchlights positioned for the defence of Loughborough. There were at least three if not four units. The accompanying guns were set up on the other side of Loughborough so that they could see any aircraft caught on the searchlights' beams instead of looking up or through the light beams. The troops attached to operate them were billeted in rooms at Bawdon Lodge Farm at Charley Crossroads. Unfortunately the best way to see the evidence is when the field has just been ploughed. I have seen these myself when ploughing the fields they stand out as mounds of red clay.

The most obvious evidence of anything still standing is to be seen in the grass field just uphill of St. Joseph's on Abbey Road where a substantial structure of brick walls can be seen. Looking rather like a shooting butt but, it is actually the remains of the building erected to house the jamming devices to counteract the German radio beams. The beams were used to guide their bombers to their targets such as the Rolls Royce engine factory in Derby, aircraft construction at Hucknall and Loughborough and the Ordnance (Ammunition) factory at Ruddington. This structure was clearly well constructed as its two-bay form with the open ends to the South is still firmly in place nearly 70 years later.

The most visible evidence of anything that the general public would have seen on a regular basis were the ammunition stores dotted along certain roads in Charnwood Forest and anywhere there was cover and camouflage provided by trees in the hedge rows. The most prominent ones were along the sides of Break-back Road between Nanpantan and Woodhouse Eaves and up Dean's Lane, also the area around the Monastery. These storage units were made out of curved corrugated steel sheets bolted together like small Nissan huts with a tarpaulin sheet hanging down to cover in both open ends. Inside were stacked ammunition boxes at least 200 to a shelter. The boxes contained 303 rifle bullets, belts of machine gun ammunition, anti-tank shells, hand grenades and smoke bombs. Some also had mortar bombs and we, as children, used to shelter in them whenever we were out in the country and it came on to rain.

Incidentally they also served to highlight the difference in the behaviour of people then and now. I do not ever remember seeing or hearing of anybody undoing any of these boxes or tampering with the stores set up for our defence. Can you imagine them being left alone today in our rotten and uncaring society where anything is considered fair game? Nevertheless, some spillage must have occurred when they were eventually removed by the army as towards the end of the war they were no longer considered necessary. Originally there had been several grouped together amongst the trees at the side of the drive leading to the Nanpantan Hall Home Farm opposite the reservoir. Now, there was a particularly dry year in the 1970's and these woods, together with those off Swanimote Road, got set on fire and the fire burnt down to the roots and dry bracken and one night the woods at Nanpantan which had been smouldering for some hours caused some anxiety and the fire brigade were sent for. Soon after their arrival explosions started to happen in the ground and they had to abandon the area and it was subsequently discovered that small arms ammunition was exploding – obviously from these old storage units.

The way these were situated along the road sides was one of two ways and usually under the shelter of trees. If the grass verge was narrow, say ten to twelve feet, then they had the ground levelled just enough for the floor area and built parallel to the road. But if a wide verge was available then several would be built at right angles especially if the road was up a hill as it was easier to level out a standing, the exception was up Dean's Lane as the verges there are very narrow so they grubbed out a short length of hedge or stone wall and extended into the field. If there happened to be a ditch on the other side they put several pipes in and then covered the area with gravel before erecting the shelter. If you look carefully these places can still be made out in Dean's Lane. They even erected some down the drive to Pocketgate and Hanging Stones Farm, also in some of the small patches of woodland.

It is possible that the building used by the scouts at Nanpantan was originally built during the war for the home guard as you will notice that it is of typical war department design as used for instance at airfields and army installations. The primary reason for having it there was for the defence of the nearby reservoir as at that time it was the main source of drinking water for Loughborough."

Michael Froggatt also had some keen observations about another special feature of wartime:

"There was another change which affected people's lives and that was the adoption of Double Summer Time and in June and July people were still out in the garden at 11 o'clock at night. Unlike today, if you ran out of anything you couldn't just go and buy some more as there probably wasn't any left and this could go on for weeks, often the shelves in shops had nothing on them and shop windows were sometimes filled with empty crates, plaster effigies of long-forgotten bananas or even crumpled newspapers. Anything to fill the space and distract the forlorn shopper from the emptiness. Everyone had to carry their identity card which could be required to be examined at any time. For the first year at least, everybody carried their gas masks wherever they went, usually in a small cardboard box hung over the shoulder, and, of course, you were always waiting for the air-raid siren to start to wail usually in the evening or at night.

One of the many pictures of Vera Lynn whose war time songs did so much to lift the spirits of the people and the military

But in typical British fashion people became used to all the restrictions and inconveniences and carried on with their daily lives until *"There'll be blue-birds over the white cliffs of Dover"* and *"the lights will come on again all over the world"* in the words of two of the most popular songs of World War 2, usually sung by Vera Lynn. Most songs and music at this time were of an optimistic nature giving people hope and encouragement with none of the country music style of today saying things like "The hens won't lay and the cow's gone dry, the crops in the field have withered and died". How depressing!"

In other chapters selected passages from the daily Chronicle kept at the Abbey have been included. Here we delve into the Chronicle for a further selection. It seems that some of the brothers in the wider movement were serving officers in the armed forces. On the 17th April 1940 it was recorded that Fr Celsus had left to become a military chaplain, and on 18th July he arrived at the Abbey for a brief stay before going off to collect tropical kit for a posting out East. On 21st July 1940 Bro. Bruno, the Naval Officer, had a call from his Commander at Birkenhead to rejoin his ship that was set to go to France.

On 8th October 1940 a Police Sergeant and a military officer came to look at Charnwood Towers (later known as Abbey Grange) as a place for military billets. Soldiers took over the building on 21st October. It turns out that their mission may well have been to guard a new secret installation being installed in the neighbouring field, referred to later as St Josephs Close.

On 27th August 1942 Brother Martin Caillard, a lay brother of Thymadeuc Abbey, France, arrived. As an English subject he had been imprisoned by the Germans in a camp near Paris, had escaped almost miraculously and tramped (in boots 2 sizes too small) to the unoccupied area. He managed to cross the border, but lacking any papers at all, was imprisoned by the French government for six weeks, until through the intervention of a bishop he was released. Travelling through France, Spain and Portugal he eventually arrived at Lisbon still wearing his lay brother's habit and then flew home. After a few days at his home he arrived at the Abbey still emaciated and far from well and was in choir the same night.

The entry for Christmas Day 1942 says that it passed away quietly. It went on: "There were no aerial activities for several days before and after the feast. Midnight Mass was offered at 3 p.m. on Christmas Eve and on the following day, by permission of the government, Christmas bells rang out all over the country between 9 a.m. and midday. This ended for us a very happy and tranquil year. Had it not been for the difficulties of the blackout and extra work on the farm, we should have scarcely known there was a war on. With the exception of a few distant raids in August we did not hear a siren during the year".

On the 1st March 1943 the Chronicler made a special entry about the nature of the winter weather. "Since November last we have had only about three cold days with not more than half an inch of snow. February in particular was a period of almost unbroken Spring weather but if the days had been fine, the nights have been hideous with the roar of scores of planes going over to bomb enemy territory. Although we have not, thank God, so much as heard a siren since last August, our raids have increased in intensity so that now we have been bombing Germany continuously day and night for a fortnight. May God have mercy on so many innocent victims.

The other entries of 1943 are all worth printing in full:

"May 30th. So improved is the international situation that the government has lifted the ban on church bell ringing provided that they are not rung in such a way as to cause alarm. Henceforth we shall ring our bells for all the day hours.

July 5th. The arrival of Francizseck Kaminski. Kaminski is a Polish solider aged about 37. After studying medicine, philosophy and theology at Louvain he entered the abbey of Lerins (Congregation of Senanque) in 1939, was drafted to the Polish army 7 months later, and eventually found himself with the Polish forces in Scotland. With some hopes of being ordained later by the Polish army Bishop Gaulina he came to spend some weeks here and was allowed to don the Oblates habit as Brother Casimir. However he was unexpectedly recalled to Glasgow and left on the 30th July after spending about three edifying weeks with us.

September 3rd. National Day of Prayer. On this day the whole nation ceased work from 11.-11.15 a.m. and listened to the service of Thanksgiving.

October 31st. Pere Marie Lacoin, formerly Procurator of Bricquebeck, but now chaplain in the Free French Navy called and stayed 24 hours.

December 30th. Although it is admitted by all that 1944 is likely to be one of the most devastating years in the world's history at least we are thankful for the unexpected peace and success of the past twelve months. Not a single raider has come our way. Almost the only sign of the war is the presence of hundreds of small ammunition dumps lining the country roads for miles around. Nine have been made on Flat Hill. Of course, the Towers, St. Joseph's Cottage and St. Joseph's Close are in the hands of the military but they are proving good tenants. This year has seen the completion of the campaigns in Africa, Sicily, and the virtual end to the U-Boat menace, Italy collapsed and largely in our hands, the recovery by Russia of nearly all her territory and such devastating raids by the RAF that the Ruhr with most of the German towns lie in ruins.

We have here Brother Christopher de Bischop, Choir Monk of Sainte Marie des Mont and Brother Martin Caillard, lay Brother of Timadeuc."

Hopefully the Chronicler's upbeat tone at the end of 1943 reflected the feeling amongst the Charley residents generally. In the next chapter we shall delve more deeply into what the Chronicler actually meant when he wrote that 'the Towers, St Joseph's Cottage and St Joseph's Close were in the hands of the military'.

During the war an increasingly obvious presence in the community were the small groups of enemy prisoners of war who were put to useful work in the countryside. Nearby Garendon had a camp, and we have already seen how a large work party from there helped with the record preparation for market of the cow cabbage plants on land near the Blackbrook Reservoir.

The Charley Heritage Group have not carried out research into what happened to the the inmates of such Prisoner of War Camps after the war. Most would have been repatriated, but some remained here and made lives in England. The group has had a very extensive conversation with Ziggy Schultz, who came to the area as a prisoner of war, and who in 2009 still lives in the Charnwood district. Ziggy's partner Marjorie Schultz is a devotee of local history studies, publishing her own book *A Layman's Guide to Garendon*. The book presents a wide range of information on the Garendon estate, the de Lisle family and the surrounding area, but there is no detail about its wartime use or its prisoner of war camp.

A tablet in the Oaks Churchyard reminds us of another such war prisoner who remained behind. Franz Stein married his Irma Kohler in 1951 and is known to have lived in Charley at One Barrow Lodge Cottage. The couple had three children. A rendering of the inscription in English has great charm.

IN LOVING MEMORY OF
FRANZ STEIN
12 11 1915 - 30 8 1993
SCHLICHT UND EINFACH
WAR DEIN LEBEN
TREU UND FLEISSIG DEINE HAND
HAST UNS ALLEN
DEINE BESTES GEGEBEN
RUH IN FREIDEN UND HAB DANK

IRMA STEIN
15 10 1921 - 22 11 2004
SEI, DER DU BIST, NICHT MEHR,
NICHT WENIGER, ABER DER SEI

Plain and simple
Was your life
Skilful and busy were your hands
You gave to all of us
Your very best
Rest in peace and many thanks

Be who you are, not more
Not less, but be it truthfully

The tablet marking the passing of Franz & Irma Stein in the Oaks Churchyard

7 ASPIRIN, BROMIDE & BENJAMIN

The Secret War Against the Luftwaffe Navigation Beams

The shelves of 21st century pharmacies have a plethora of pills that deal with many of the aches and pains that afflict us in our daily lives. That was not the case back in wartime. In the 1940s, most people then would associate *aspirin* as being the remedy for a *headache*. That word headache can have a number of interpretations, and the sense of it meaning an annoyingly difficult problem to solve is the basis used in this chapter.

The term *ruffian* can be understood to mean an unruly, hard to pin down sort of character. One remedy is to give a ruffian a sedative, a draught of *bromide*, to calm him down and remove the worst of his behaviour. More about this and the meaning of *Benjamin* as the story unfolds.

In 1940, after the Germans abandoned plans for the invasion of the British Isles, they turned the might of the Luftwaffe bomber fleet onto targeting our industrial capacity and civilian morale. Massed night-time bombing raids became the norm and the ways of combating them greatly exercised the minds of the war cabinet. We had not yet developed the capacity to put up a squadron of aircraft that could operate as night interceptors to harass and destroy the bombers en route. Searchlights, balloons and ground based anti-aircraft guns were the primary defence tools.

It became apparent that the invading bomber forces were using a special plan involving a lead group of bombers to identify the target. This group's primary bomb load was incendiary devices intended to create massive fires at the target area. The main bomber force following a little later would then have the fire zone to guide them into the target. It also became apparent that the lead bomber group seemed to be able to find their target with unerring accuracy in the dark, and all the bombers seemed to be able to find their way home with some precision.

The situation was certainly a great *headache* to the war cabinet, and we could be said to be being plagued by this horde of unstoppable *ruffians*. One man came to spearhead the response to this situation, Dr R V Jones, who as a scientist had been attached to Air Intelligence since the outbreak of the war. His special remit was to investigate new techniques being used in air warfare by the Germans. All the work that stemmed from this relationship was deemed top secret, and nobody outside those involved ever knew the detail until the 30 year rule expired in 1975, and the then Professor Jones was able to publish his story, *Most Secret War, British Scientific Intelligence, 1939-1945*, Hamish Hamilton, London 1978. One of the units that resulted from Dr Jones' initiatives was the top secret No. 80 Signals Wing of the Royal Air Force with its headquarters at Radlett in Hertfordshire, and outstations at many places in England, including one right in the centre of our very own Charley. An outstanding account of the history of this unit was published in 1997 entitled *Royal Air Force Beam Benders, No. 80 Signals Wing 1940-1945*, Laurie Brettingham, Midland Publishing, Leicester.

Dr R V Jones

From his book, Most Secret War

It is a typically British story. A seemingly maverick boffin coming up with a novel take on a deeply technical development, and the reactionary old guard in power scoffing at his ideas. It took the indomitable spirit and vision of the Prime Minister, Winston Churchill, to give Dr Jones' work the primacy it deserved, and install him at the heart of the war cabinet's response to the air war. Air Intelligence worked on standard methods, bringing together many seemingly small and disparate pieces of information, so that they could be pondered over as a whole. And so it was that onto the desk at Air Intelligence came secretly recorded conversations between captured German aircrew mentioning the *X-gerat* or *X-apparatus*; and then extra-sensitive blind landing receivers found in downed Luftwaffe aircraft were noted; the words *Radio Beacon Knickerbein from 0600 hours on 315 deg* found on a scrap of paper in a crashed plane; a decoded Enigma intercept linking the name Knickerbein, the German town of Kleve and some co-ordinates linking Kleve with Retford in Nottinghamshire; all contributed to the framework building in Dr Jones' mind. He came to believe that the Germans had developed a system of narrow radio beams that enemy bombers could follow to a point where two beams intersected over a target, and then also to use one of the beams to return home.

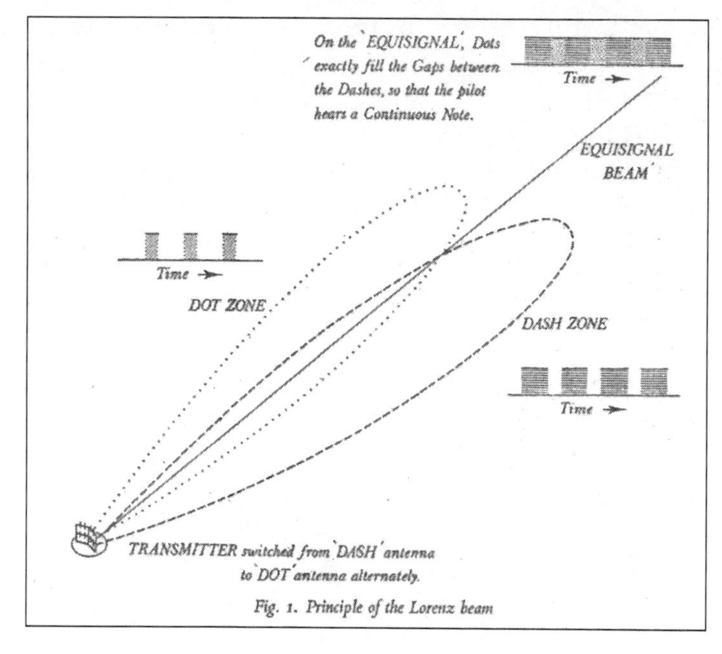

Fig. 1. Principle of the Lorenz beam

The diagram from Most Secret War.

P.98

Dr Jones reasoned that the hotted-up Lorenz-type blind landing receiver found in the crashed Heinkel III was working with a very strong and focused beam from Germany or France. Typically in a blind landing the aircrew would hear a series of dots if their aircraft was off the approach line to one side, or dashes if off to other side. Because the pulses in the two beams were alternately phased, when the aircraft was on the centre line where the two beams overlapped, the dots and dashes interweaved to give a continuous tone. A German aircraft heading for a pre-determined target in England would track the Knickerbein beam in the same way. Dr Jones also reasoned that there had to be two beams; the second beam crossing the first at the target, the so-called 'crooked leg'. Another piece of paper came across the Air Intelligence desk, this time from a German aircraft shot down in France. This identified the position, frequencies and co-ordinates of both Kleve, and Bredstedt in Schleswig Holstein, as sources of the two beams.

Now Dr Jones had to prove the existence of these Knickerbein beams and on 18th and 20th June 1940 a search aircraft was sent up with a special crew and equipment to prove the theory, but no beams were detected. On 21st June Dr Jones was summoned to 10 Downing Street to a specially convened and very secret meeting on the threat posed by the beams. The top brass around the table were a mixture of the out of touch, uninformed and dismissive, but Dr Jones' 20 minute review of the situation convinced Churchill, if not all those present, of the solid possibilities for the German deployment and use of beams. Churchill was told that provided the beams were detected, countermeasures could include anything from creating false and misleading beams right through to outright jamming. Churchill let it be known that he wanted the work to continue.

Back down to earth in Air Intelligence that afternoon there was a Signals conference. It came round to the Knickerbein beam from Kleve, and an expert adviser T L Eckersley generally rubbished the science that Dr Jones was relying on. In consequence, the Deputy Director of Signals, Group Captain Lywood, voiced his intention not to waste any more effort on detecting beams and to therefore cancel that night's beam detector flight.

Sure of his own interpretation of the science, and with much other evidence, Dr Jones was horrified that the search for the beams would stop. He played a trump card, telling Lywood that Churchill himself that day had authorised that night's search flight, and that Churchill would be told who had personally countermanded his orders, if the flight was called off. Lywood backed down.

Here Dr Jones made the crucial and fateful decision. When asked where the aircraft should look for the beam signal, he reasoned that the most important target in England for the Luftwaffe to focus on was the Rolls Royce plant in Derby where the Merlin engine was built, just a short way north of Charley. So on that night Flight Lt. Bufton and Corporal Mackie flew north from Wyton in Huntingdonshire without being told about Knickerbein, but simply to look for a Lorenz type beam and find the equi-signal line. Bufton & Mackie found themselves crossing the two beams as they flew on their northerly track, and it is very likely that at some time during that flight Bufton turned west and flew along the beam towards Derby, with the brooding mass of Charnwood on his left.

At the debriefing next day, Bufton delivered this report, taken here as an image from page 104 of Dr Jones' book, Most Secret War.

> (1) That there is a narrow beam (approximately 400–500 yards wide), passing through a position 1 mile S. of Spalding, having dots to the south and dashes to the north, on a bearing of 104°–284°T.
> (2) That the carrier frequency of the transmissions on the night of 21/22 June was 31·5 Mc/sec. modulated at 1150 cycles and similar to Lorenz characteristics.
> (3) That there is a second beam having similar characteristics but with dots to the north and dashes to the south synchronized with the southern beam, apparently passing through a point near Beeston on a bearing lying between 60°+ and less than 104°.

There was now no doubt, the turning point had been reached. The task of developing countermeasures led to the formation of a very specialised and secret unit, No 80 (Signals) Wing, Royal Air Force, with its own headquarters at Radlett, in Herfordshire.

From there a set of links was established with outstations at strategic points from which all sorts of clever science was deployed. One such outstation was positioned in Charley itself, right under the paths of beams laid onto possible targets in the West Midlands, Derbyshire and South Yorkshire.

The Insignia of 80 Wing and its brilliant leader, Air Vice Marshall E B Addison CB CBE

From RAF Beam Benders

Alongside Knickerbein, codenamed Headache, and increasingly instead of it because of its usefulness being interfered with by 80 Signals Wing, the Germans deployed X-Gerat, the *Ruffians* of 80 Signals codespeak. Initially developed for use by KGr 100, the Luftwaffe's specialised Pathfinder & Fireraiser squadron, flying out of Vannes on the Brest Peninsula, it introduced another level of sophistication. KGr 100 aircraft would navigate down a beam towards the target before coming over cross beams which in conjunction with clocks and precise identification of aircraft speed, would indicate the bomb release point. This precision was potentially devastating, since KGr 100's task was to set huge fires at the target so that other parts of the bomber force could easily see the target in the dark. 80 Signals Wing developed the *Bromide* response to the Ruffians threat.

Ever resourceful, the Germans introduced yet another type of beam system, the Y-Gerat, codenamed Benito, after Mussolini. This was a single beam, with a system of pulses back and forth between the aircraft and an active controller at the beam source

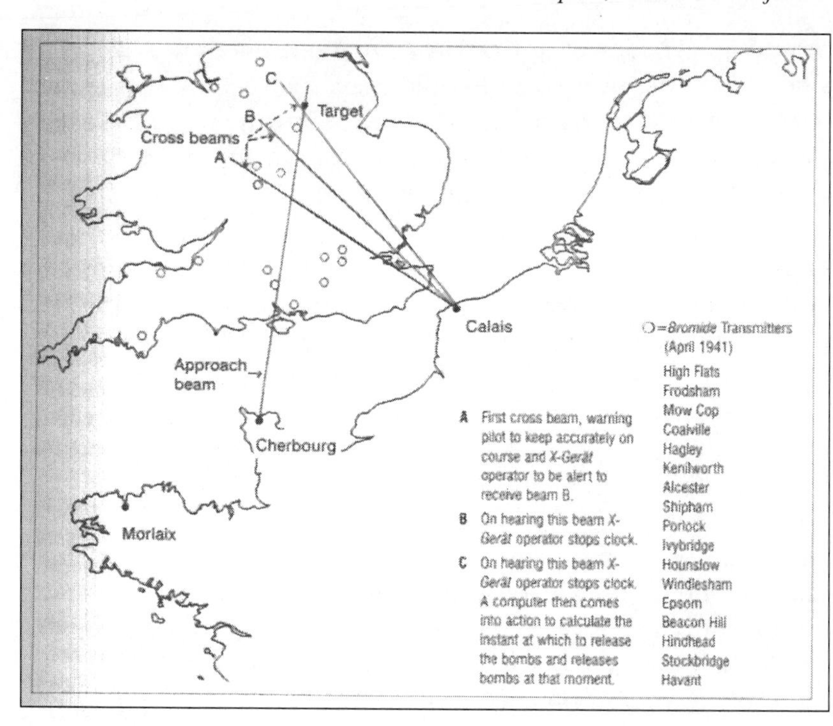

The scheme of the X-Gerat System

From RAF Beam Benders P.19

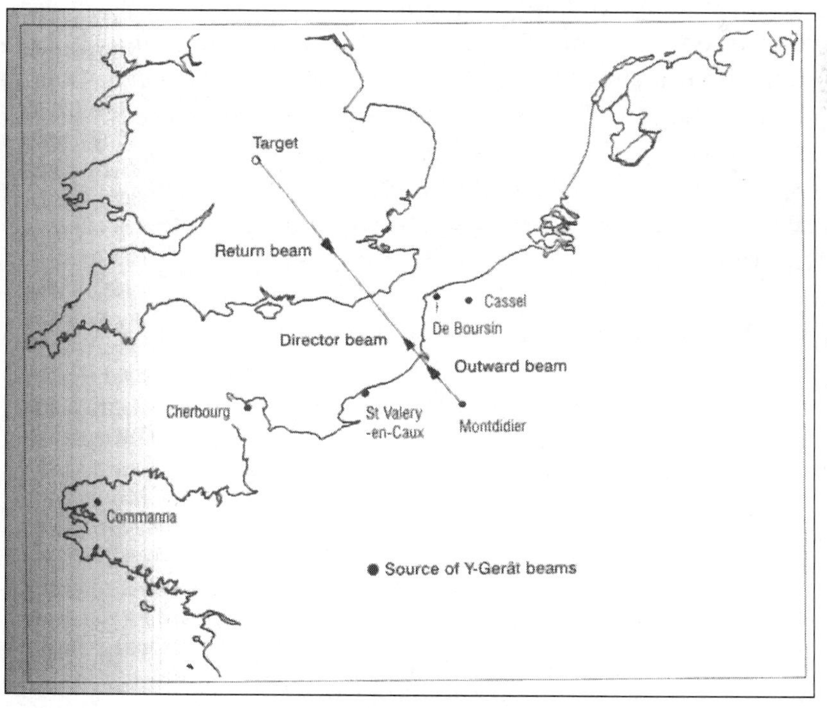

The scheme of the Y-Gerat System

From RAF Beam Benders P.23

in France. The idea was that the active controller knew precisely where the aircraft was, and could issue instructions as to when to discharge the bomb load. It relied on the use of a visual display in the cockpit and by the controller, using an oscilloscope. Domino transmitters were initially used to confuse or jam the signals, but the main response by 80 Signals Wing was codenamed Benjamin. There are no clues in the literature as to why Benjamin was chosen. Perhaps it was nothing more complicated that a conflation of the two words, *Benito Jamming*. It was always important to use these codenames rather than the real German names, so that our access to the Enigma coded messages was not compromised.

The nature of the response to the three threats, Headache, Bromide and Benito, was not a wholesale jamming. In a much more subtle approach, techniques were developed to mask the signals coming from the German beacons. In essence, the signals would be copied and re-radiated but in a way that rendered them unreliable to the aircrews, who could not distinguish the re-radiated signals as not being their own. In the vernacular, the term Beam Bending came into use, but this is not an accurate summary of the interference done to the German transmissions. The term *Masking* of *Beacons* became *Meaconing* in the working jargon of 80 Signals Wing. The machines and equipment used for this purpose at the outstations became *Meacons*, Aspirin for the Headaches, Bromide for the Ruffians, and Benjamin for Benito. The Charley outstation had all three types of equipment.

So what was happening in Charley at its Outstation of 80 Wing, and how was it controlled from Radlett? Clearly the high ground of Charley was one precondition for the siting of a Meacon station. Another was its position under the likely track of beams aimed at midlands industrial centres. But where in particular to site the station? The Monastery Community at the Abbey owned many acres up on the high ground, but probably most meaningfully had a neat little enclosure next to two access roads, which was called St Joseph's Field. Since these Outstations of 80 Wing were always fairly makeshift, quick to be set up or dismantled, the field was settled on. The Abbott agreed, and the

RAF located its Coalville Outstation on that field, putting in its transmitters; one Aspirin, two Bromides, and two Benjamins. Corroborating evidence of the use of this field emerges by looking carefully at the local map drawn up by the War Agriculture Committee referred to in chapter 4. Here we reproduce the portion of the map centred on St Joseph's Field. All the land around is allocated to the relevant farms, but the corner containing Charnwood Towers, St Joseph's Cottage, and the field in between is not allocated to anybody. The field itself has been picked out with single dashes with a legend that looks like 'NON AGL', which probably translates as 'Non Agricultural'. The OS has also stamped *BM 570* in the field, which means there is a benchmark location at 570 feet above sea level.

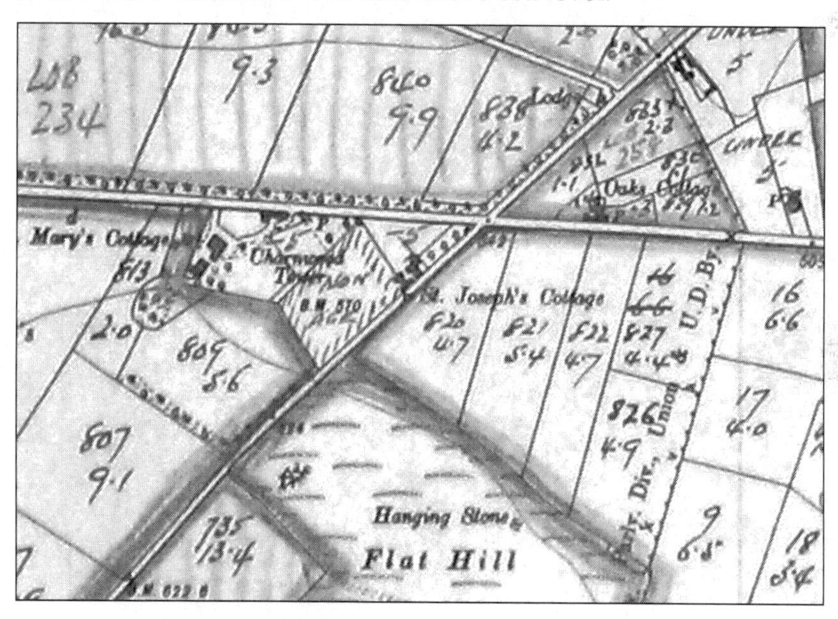

The Air 540 listing on the next two pages implies that this highly secret installation was operational from 25 November 1940. It has been possible to interview an RAF Wireless Mechanic who served on this site for almost two years. Ken Nicholls, now a resident of Coalville, confirms the makeshift arrangements at the site. The Benjamin transmitter work was carried out in equipment housed in a trailer, parked inside a brick blast wall enclosure still standing in 2009. The others were in hastily erected sectional sheds arranged along the western edge of the

21793 Wt. 38805/3593 400,000 12/39—McC & Co—51-5658

R.A.F. Form 540

See instructions for use of this form in K.R. and A.C.I., para. 2349, and War Manual, Pt. II., chapter XX., and notes in R.A.F. Pocket Book.

OPERATIONS

of (Unit or Formation)

(1)	(2)	(3)	(4)	(5)
NORTHERN AREA	(Continued).			
ST[illegible]	[illegible].8.40	20. 5. [illegible]	Watcher	
DRONE [illegible]	14.8.40.	1.5. [illegible].	Watcher.	
[illegible]	1. 5. [illegible]	1. 5.41.	Watcher.	
HAR[illegible]	27.11.40.	9. 4.41.	Watcher.	
SCHOOL HILL.	13. 8. 40.	30.11.40.	Watcher.	
DOUGLAS WOOD.	-. 7.40.	-.10.41.	Watcher.	
MILLINGTON			Aspirin.	
			MIDLAND	AREA
COALVILLE	25.11.40.	-	Aspirin Bromide " Benjamin	Peto-Scott G.M.C. G.M.C. G.E.C. G.E.C.
HAGLEY Area Headquarters.	11.9.40.	-	Aspirin " Bromide "	S.T.& C. S.T.& C. G.M.C. G.M.C.
KENILWORTH	[illegible].40	-	Bromide Aspirin	G.M.C. G.M.C.

Page 70 of the records of RAF 80 Wing (Signals) from class reference AIR 540 at the Public Record Office at Kew. The document is split over these two pages

RECORD BOOK Page No. 70

No. of pages used for day

		APPENDIX No.	PAGE
(6)	(7)	(8)	(9)
		Moved to Louth.	
		Moved to Ayton.	
		Moved to Ayton.	
		Naval.	
		Closed down.	
		Closed down.	
		Awaiting transmitters.	T.U.4., Diathermy from Market Weighton.
30. 1. 41. 25.11.40. 14.12.40. 6. 7.41. 6.7.42.			
11.9.40. 24.10.40. 1.11.40. 25.11.40.			
7.11.40. 8. 5.41.			G.H.Q.

field. In the centre was a larger shed, the domain of the RAF Sergeant who was in charge of the site, and his Corporal. He had a stove, and kept a stock of the radio equipment spares that they needed. The Sergeant was from an administrative background, not a wireless tradesman. The unit's complement of wireless mechanics was around twelve, and there was an RAF Policeman to keep an eye on security. They were almost all very young, and lived in lodgings in Shepshed, save for one mechanic who had the good fortune to be posted right next to his home town, Loughborough. He went home at the end of his shift. The mechanics crewed a 24hr three-shift operation, though most of their activity took place at night, when the German bomber forces were usually at large. There were no Officers at the unit in St Joseph's Field or next door in the Cottage.

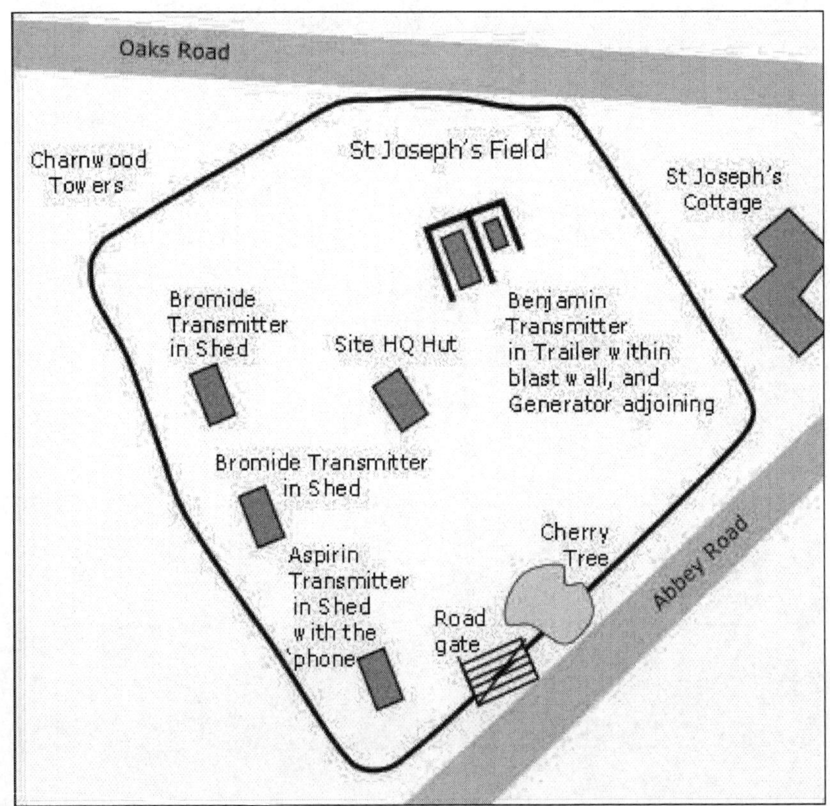

The Layout of the Coalville Outstation in the mind of Ken Nicholls

The makeshift set up of the site is born out by some of the arrangements that were or were not made. Electric power came from diesel powered generator sets on small trailers parked alongside each transmitter housing. The all important telephone line linking the site to Radlett was housed in the shed containing the Aspirin transmitter. There would always be a Wireless Mechanic on duty there. There were no arrangements for meals, the crews bringing in lunch packs from their digs, though they could make a brew. The toilet was of the earth closet variety, inside a small shed, which was periodically moved about the field. No grass cutting was carried out, the mechanics forging well trodden paths through the meadow.

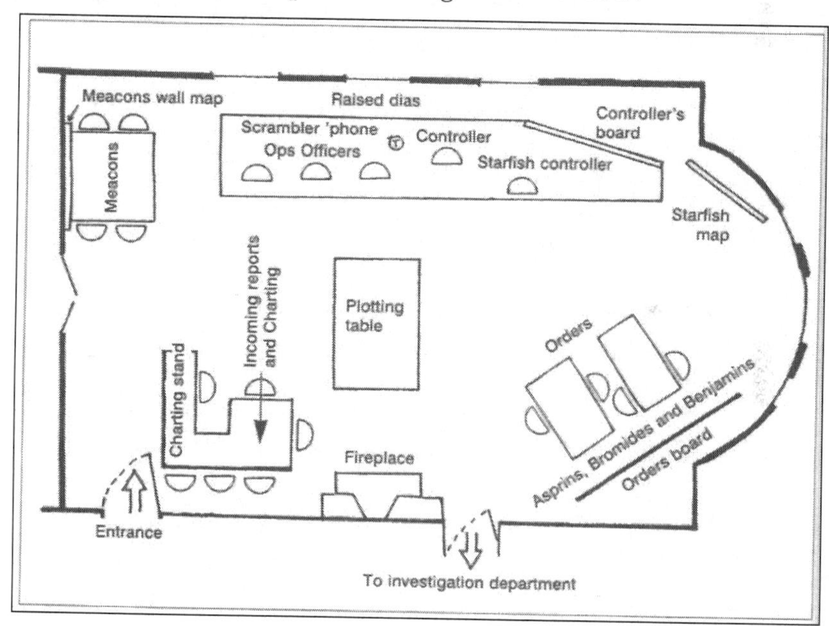

The Ops Room at 80 Wing HQ Radlett

From RAF Beam Benders P.32

So it was on impromptu sites like this, located in fields about the country, that one arm of the fight against the German bomber force did its valuable stuff. The diagrams of the Radlett Headquarter setup give a clue as to how the system was controlled. Its telephone links were given absolute priority over all other traffic. All sorts of intelligence flowed into the Ops Room to be digested and decisions taken on action. Typically, as the people of Charley slept in their beds at night in the winter of 1940 and through 1941 and 1942, a call would come through to St Josephs Field from Radlett with the curt instructions such as *switch on your Bromides* to counter a very current looming bombing attack. This activity was generally referred to as *Meaconing*, typically taking on the form of clearly tuning in to the incoming enemy signal, and then re-radiating it from the outstation's transmitters. The effect on the enemy aircrew was either to mask out the clarity of their beam, or to subtly shift its line, a sort of 'bending'.

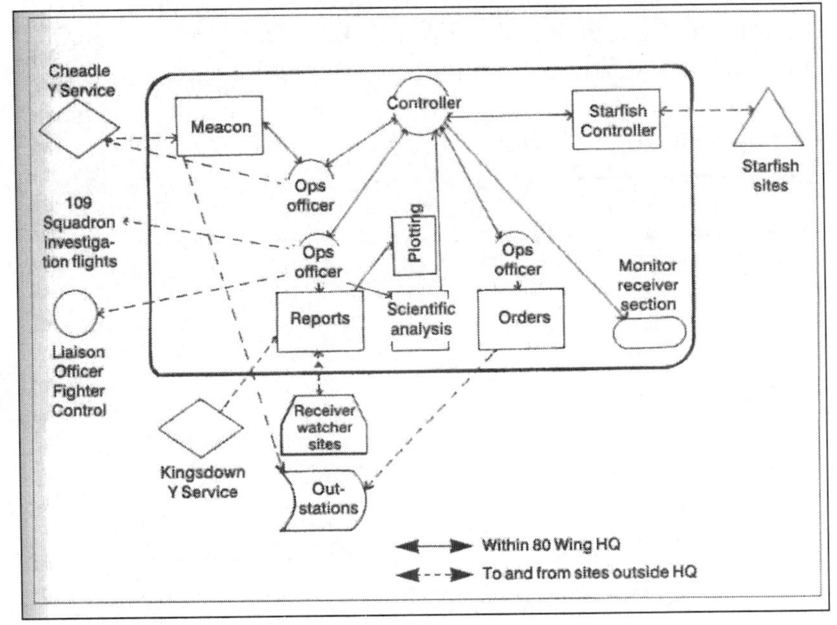

The Flow Diagram for the Ops Room at 80 Wing HQ Radlett

From RAF Beam Benders P.37

For his 1997 book *Beam Benders* Laurie Brettingham collected oral testimony from many of the actual operators who worked at the outstations, and prints their words in the book. He was clearly unable to find anybody to talk about life at St Josephs. So to give an idea we print here an account of operator activity from the book at page 149. George Morle was posted to the out station at Beacon Hill, Wiltshire, on the high ground behind Bulford Army Camp. Here is his account of a typical activity.

> George Morle(Beacon Hill, Wiltshire: Parliament Hill, London)
> "1 volunteered for the RAF in 1940. I was already a wireless operator but did a wireless course at Compton Bassett, in Wiltshire. After this I was posted to No. 80

Wing. My first introduction to Radlett was the reception at HQ on arrival, a 'pep' talk on secrecy, followed by the clearance procedure after which I was transferred back to Wiltshire, to Beacon Hill, being taken there in a small van from Radlett. My billet was in Bulford, three miles away, and the van took me there. The billet was a cottage on the outskirts of the village. The local police sergeant told me later he had great difficulty persuading these folk to take me in, he hoped it would work out alright. Getting to the radio station at Beacon Hill would take nearly an hour being uphill all the way. I had my cycle sent from London but it was only useful for the ride down.

Beacon Hill is the high ground behind Bulford Army Camp; it was a site for the original beacon warning of the Armada 400 years ago. In 1941 it was enclosed with barbed wire and guarded by the Army. One side of the hill was covered by several mobile vans and two huts, each housing a transmitter. The vans were converted furniture vans which had previously been used along the south coast to try and locate the enemy beams. The site was a hive of activity. Post Office Engineers working with TRE (Telecommunications Research Establishment) personnel from Worth Matravers, Swanage, were installing equipment on a permanent basis, working up, as they said, "From bits of string to solid state!". On the far side of the hill was another, smaller hut, the Receiver Hut, my place of work. On the job training started immediately, (radio counter-measures against Y-Gerat).

The receiver hut was the heart of the job. It controlled the whole operation. The receivers were Hallicrafters 521 and there were two main positions along one side of the hut, each with a receiver and a control unit containing a cathode ray tube. TRE had fitted an antenna balance unit on the roof inside the hut, so that our own transmitter did not swamp us during transmission. The 521 receiver had a large dial, covering both the 30

MHz and 40 MHz band, and it could be difficult to get an accurate reading... Eventually we were supplied with wavemeters to check our readings, but this took many months to happen.

When a German ground station came on the air (usually Cherbourg or Cassel in France), we would report the signal 'on' and order our own transmitter to power up to 'standby', and awaited orders from Radlett. There would be flying time before the aircraft crossed the coast en route for the target. Meanwhile a beam station would come up on a different frequency. The signal was checked, the speed of the dashes counted and reported. If it was a big operation other stations would be logged in a similar way. Ground stations would call their aircraft giving us a lead to call signs to be used. If in our range these would be picked up on the wide band receiver on 47 MHz. When in the target area the ground station would transmit further signals which we re-radiated. This was also an indication that we would soon hear the 'drop-bombs' signal, which took the form of an exaggerated S0S sounding like three dashes followed by long dashes and three dashes. This was so distinctive and important that our reaction was immediate and we used our Morse keys to jam the signal. The excitement and tension is hard to explain. We would also receive either Morse or speech from the Germans, all logged from beginning to end.

The Army guards were friendly and got used to our odd hours of coming and going. On quiet nights one of us went off duty about 2am. Many times I passed through the camp unchallenged but one night I was attacked by a guard. I shouted loudly and he backed off. we monitored, measured, counted, but to no avail. Eventually, after the famous commando raid on Bruneval on the French Coast, where a German radar station was dismantled and the equipment brought back to Britain, we lost our signal without explanation."

Our very own Wireless Mechanic, Leading Aircraftsman Ken Nicholls, drew on a rich seam of stories from his time in St Joseph's Field in his interview for this book. Born at Lye in Worcestershire in 1923, he volunteered for the Royal Air Force as soon as he was 18. Missing out on becoming aircrew because of an ear problem, Ken opted to train as a Wireless Mechanic. "I thought it would be something I could get interested in", he recounted. After a six-months course at Bolton College Ken took up his posting to the Coalville Outstation of No. 80 Signals Wing. "I came by train from Bolton, finished up at Loughborough", he remembers. "Then a bus to Shepshed. I'd been told where my digs were, because we were all out in private digs. So I arrived at this house in Shepshed, in Glenmore Avenue. I think it was No. 12, and I think it was a Mr & Mrs Cook, who were very good to me. I left my kitbag and the associated stuff and found my way up to the site, which was a long walk".

Leading Aircraftsman Ken Nicholls, and his coveted Wireless Mechanic Badge

Ken Nicholls had only experienced a short spell of military style discipline during his basic training, or *square bashing* in popular parlance. The St Joseph's site was very unmilitary, and the visiting top people from Radlett added to his impression that he was working for civilians. Ken puts it like this. “The people that were responsible, that were in charge of 80 Wing, were not RAF personnel as such. They were in the RAF but they were what I refer to as boffins. They had been brought into the RAF so that in effect, it was controlled by civilians who happened to be in RAF uniform, which is rather different from the normal practice where RAF people are in charge”.

When on duty with his three other shiftmates, the crew would usually be located in the Aspirin building, the Peto Scott transmitter, with the telephone in the corner. When it rang, Ken relates the action they took. “What Radlett usually did...they were usually able to give us a little bit of notice so we’d run the transmitters up because it could take anything from 10 to 15 minutes to get it up on air. We would then wait for them to send us the frequency. They would then send the frequency and we had to set it up on that particular frequency, and then we’d beam it out, just blast it out actually, not beam it”.

It was difficult for those young airmen in St Joseph’s Field to have any idea as to how well they were doing. It was a secret silent Battle of the Beams almost in the realm of science fiction. Ken Nicholls sums up a view about effectiveness with a reference to the mistaken raid on Dublin in May 1941. “We always reckoned that we were responsible in part for the bombing of Dublin. I don't know why we should take credit for that, other than perhaps diverting them from Liverpool. It was difficult really to know. It wasn't difficult for the people in charge to know. Because, from the beam, they knew where the target was. They knew for example that the target might be Birmingham, and if the bombers came over, at night, and instead of bombing Birmingham, they bombed some oat fields near Coalville, they knew they had achieved something, because they had possibly taken them off course”.

There are many accounts in the Brettingham book where captured airmen confessed to being ‘hopelessly lost’, a direct result of the meaconing activity of 80 Signals Wing. Brettingham also quotes from German war diary material that has subsequently emerged. As the Benjamin meaconing activity became effective, it was often the case that the ground controllers lost their ability to pinpoint their aircraft, and ordered the crews to find their own way into their mission. A further development controlled by Radlett was the programme of *Starfish* sites. These were areas where huge fires could be started deliberately in open country to hoodwink incoming bomber formations into dropping their bombs harmlessly on these fake targets. There was a large Starfish site in the Vale of Belvoir, on the way in towards those vital factories in Derby.

So Charley was right up there in this immensely important yet secret battle against the might of the Luftwaffe bomber force. Nobody local knew what was going on in that field next to St Josephs, not then, nor for many years after the war ended. Fortunately for us, the likes of Dr R V Jones and the scientific community were on the case, and Wing Commander Addison's 80 Signals Wing displayed great attention to detail in their unceasing application of those Aspirins, Bromides and Benjamins. And even more fortunately, much of the enemy bomber force was re-directed at Russia later in 1941, away from our shores. And so some of the *Headaches* went, the *Ruffians* showed up much less often, and *Benito* did not pose the threat it once did. The 'beam bender' brickwork next to St Josephs remains as a reminder of those most dangerous times, and that amazing enterprise.

But there is one more enduring and wonderful thing that emerged from that wartime field of St Josephs. Ken Nicholls tells of a day in 1942 when he and his shiftmate were taking a rest with a mug of tea, leaning on the gate that gave access to Abbey Road, under a particularly fruitful cherry tree. Coming up the hill from the Shepshed direction were two young women, pushing their cycles rather than attempting the climb in the saddle. The 19-year old Ken Nicholls took an instant liking to one of the girls, with the result that she agreed to take up his offer to meet at a dance in Coalville. Iris Hardy had been on a visit to an aunt in Shepshed, and was on her way home to Ellistown. The meeting in the dance hall began to cement the relationship, and Ken Nicholls' off-duty time became a new set of very precious interludes with his Iris. When much later, with the war with Germany finished, and Ken having received notice of posting to the Far East, Ken & Iris decided to get married before he left. With both their parents to witness the ceremony, the two joined their lives together at Ellistown Church on 6th August 1945. That of course was the day the nuclear bomb was exploded over Hiroshima. An 80 Wing radar jamming unit was not needed in the Far East after that. Demobilisation followed in the October, and Ken & Iris were able to build a family and a life in North West Leicestershire, lived out so close to that field in St Josephs were they first chanced upon each other.

Ken Nicholls JP, in 2009, when interviewed for this book

8 REFLECTIONS ON THE PEACE

The Modern Links to the Girl Born in 1940

Through the recent change of Millennium and since, a dining table in St Joseph's Cottage at The Oaks cross roads has been the frequent haunt of the band of enthusiasts who call themselves the Charley Heritage Group. Round this table, and sometimes in other houses, they have pieced together the past, put bits of it down in books, and created Charley's very own Millennium map. They have sat down with a tape recorder in front of some local characters with long memories and fascinating stories to tell. And then one day in early 2008 they sat down at that table to hear a special announcement from their Chairperson. Sitting at the head of the table was Maureen Havers, alongside her husband John, who looks after the Group's purse. "We've got our Award, the bid was successful", was all that she said.

Everybody cheered. Not content with the work the Group had accomplished so far, it had put in a bid for Lottery money to fund an ambitious project dreamed up by the Group. They now had the money to buy archival and display equipment, stage an exhibition *Charley Through The Ages*, publish a website, carry out a programme of video recording to be edited into a DVD *Charley Through The Seasons*, and publish a book *World War II in Charley*.

This is that very book, and as the work on it progressed, the significance of some of the connections has gradually dawned. As the group members found their way up the rear drive into St Josephs for their meetings, and parked their cars next to the hedgeline into the neighbouring field, they began to tune in to what was happening in that field in 1941 and 1942. There a keen little bunch of hardly militarised RAF types had occupied themselves with the secret business of the RAF's No. 80 Wing, as its Coalville outstation. Scattered about that field then were the Aspirin, Bromide and Benjamin transmitters in their rudimentary sheds and trailer ready to be deployed on beam jamming operations on the call from 80 Wing headquarters at Radlett. Movingly, the blastwall enclosure built to shelter the Benjamin transmitter and its generator still remains, and serves to remind today's group members of that intriguing past.

An almost unbelievable connection is that John & Maureen Havers should be the then tenants of St Joseph's House in 2008, as the book was being planned. Unbelievable in that this Maureen Havers is the Maureen Ridley of Chapter 2 who was born in Coventry in an air raid in August 1940; whose parents moved away with her shortly afterwards to Ilkley; whose Coventry house was destroyed in the massive raid on Coventry in that November; and without any knowledge of this, the now married Maureen with her family left Coventry in 1981 to take up the Abbey's offer of the tenancy of St Josephs.

Chapter 2 describes how Maureen, then resident at St Josephs, got to know Charlie Brooks, who built Hillside Bungalow on the lane near the site of the Reformatory. In her conversation with Charlie she heard his emotional account of watching the distant fires in Coventry from the vantage point near the Bungalow, the very fires that had consumed the house where she was born in Coventry. And the connections go on. Charlie has now died, and the opportunity for Maureen and John to take up residence in that bungalow was offered. Since St Josephs has the room and space for a big family, and the bungalow is cosy and snug, Maureen and John moved into the Bungalow, completing this amazing circle of connections.

Perhaps because Charley is a small rural parish, with relatively few dwellings scattered about over the Forest, it invites a close understanding of why things are how they are, and how they came to be where and how they are. This curiosity is more easily satisfied because of the small and scattered nature of the place. The enquirer can actually get their head round the provenance.

It is also a beautiful and sometimes wild place, which inspires and encourages the search for understanding.

The Charley Heritage Group hopes that this book will anchor in print a record of what it was like here in the years of World War II. The interested reader could discover more of the day to day life of wartime Charley by spending a morning in Loughborough Library reading through the Loughborough Echo. We were only able to study a sample year of 1940 for this book. The keener reader may want to follow up the amazing secret work of the RAF 'Beambenders', of Chapter 7. The two books mentioned there are a great read.

At the end of the war in May 1945 the Loughborough Echo was full of accounts of marches, celebrations, street parties and a myriad ways of enjoying the feeling of having defeated the enemy. As the Allies advanced into Germany there were a steady number of articles in 1945 about servicemen who had been freed from prisoner of war camps. Entries in the paper under the heading Oaks in Charnwood were often absent each week. When it came to the issue of 11th May 1945, with many fulsome reports of celebrations and parties in many villages, the brief report for The Oaks struck a quieter tone. We reproduce the entry here. Perhaps the floor of the Parish Room really rocked that night to the tapping of many happy feet.

OAKS-IN-CHARNWOOD
The victory celebrations at the
Oaks included a service on
VE-Day, a peal of bells and a
dance in the Parish Room.

Although life took on a new sense of hope and relief now that peace had come, many of the privations of wartime were still with us. Most needs were in short supply. Food, clothing, furniture and road fuel remained rationed. Charley residents were all too aware of that other reminder of war, the roadside ammunition stores that could be seen along many forest roads. A general sense of clamour arose in the whole area as to why the stores had not been moved away, and a keen interest in when it might happen. So much so that the Army Command responsible held a great public meeting and press conference at its headquarters at Garendon Hall in January 1946. In its issue of January 18th 1946, The Loughborough Echo published a detailed report of the proceedings.

AMMUNITION DUMPS NEAR
LOUGHBOROUGH
TO REMAIN ANOTHER YEAR
Questions answered at Press Conference

So ran the headline. Chief Ordnance Officer, Colonel L H Jackson, OBE, RAOC, stated some facts:

- there was no possibility whatever of the ammunition being removed within the next twelve months
- as the ammunition is moved it is taken for disposal
- transport for ammunition takes second place to food and coal
- tampering and pilfering has increased in recent months
- the ammunition is not dangerous if not interfered with.

Colonel Jackson was rigorously questioned and all sorts of interesting information emerged in the answers. Loughborough had been selected as the centre for ammunition stockpiling because it was in the centre of England close to lots of country lanes with wide verges and the convenient railhead of Quorn. Cheap steel shelters in such locations would not spoil the future landscape, and the need for providing guards from men needed for war service was deemed unnecessary. Country people's good sense would be the best guards. The stocks in place all around Loughborough were huge, considerably more than 'hundreds of thousands of tons'. Col. Jackson assured the people present that all stored ammunition would eventually be taken away for disposal, though recently it had been found expeditious to discharge quantities of smoke generators on site. He explained that Beacon Hill had been nominated for this work, which explained the mystery of the dense smoke emanating from the Beacon, causing many people to believe that the countryside was on fire.

And so the smoke of war cleared, and the Spring returned again in 1946. The sun shone through the clouds, and rainbows once again visited Charley parish, the hidden jewel of Charnwood Forest.

The so called 'Beam Bender' structure that still sits in St Joseph's Field, as drawn for Charley's Millennium Map. It has no useful purpose in 2009, attracting its own patch of nettles and assorted weeds. Perhaps it does serve to remind us of those days when war was fought in mysterious ways with unseen radio signals and flying machines laden with armaments too awful to contemplate.

A typical wartime scene in the fields of Charley

APPENDIX
The 1941 Farm Survey

Extracts from the detailed records held
at the National Archives at Kew.

Records:
MAF 32/379
135

Maps:
MAF 73/22
24 & 27

The front entrance to the enlarged National Archives building at Kew, in 2009

There were 24 farms listed in the 1941 National Farm Survey within the civil parish of Charley. The parish based files at the Public Record Office at Kew typically have three sheets with five sides.

Sheet 1 is two sided. On the front it bears the addressograph generated address of the farmer, and the return address when folded. On the reverse side is Form CC47/S.S.Y, the RETURN WITH RESPECT TO AGRICULTURAL LAND ON 4TH JUNE 1941. This yields data on the acreage of crops grown, livestock, labour and working horses.

Sheet 2 is single sided and also dated June 1941, headed SF, yielding additional data on labour, on motive power used on the farm, the type of tenancy and rental paid, and the length of occupation.

Sheet 3 is the formal typewritten double sided FARM SURVEY Form No. B496/E.I. prepared by a named Inspector and dated during the early part of 1942. This document gives detailed data about ownership, tenure, the condition of all the elements of the holding, the supply of utilities and then applies a Grade to the quality of the management. On the reverse are spaces for General Comments, and for comments headed Grass Fields Ploughed Up, both for 1940 and for 1941.

Examples of all these returns are printed in the beginning of the appendix for Farm No. 135/1. For the other 23 farms, we have included just the addressograph plate image.

The authorities further documented each holding by marking out in colour the territory on OS sheet maps. Each farm's territory was given a number preceded by the code letters for the district. Charley's farms were in the Loughborough district, so the territory of William Blackett's Vale Farm No. 135/1 can be located on the maps with the code LOB 209. Inserts from the maps are printed with each entry in this Appendix.

All the map prints have been rendered in grayscale, without colour.

1

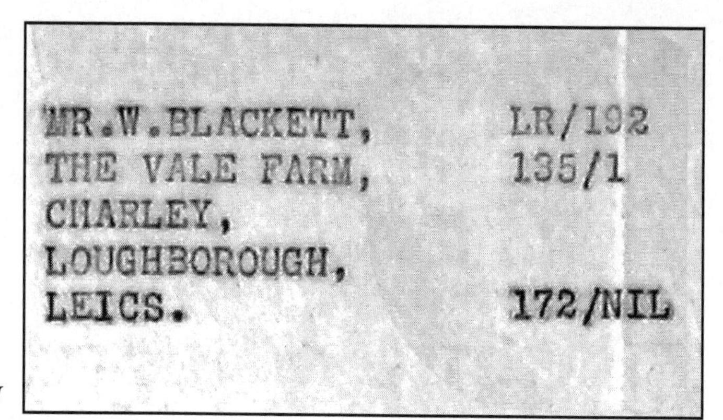

MR.W.BLACKETT, LR/192
THE VALE FARM, 135/1
CHARLEY,
LOUGHBOROUGH,
LEICS. 172/NIL

Map 24 NW
246 acres
Map Code LOB 209 Also includes Hall Farm Graded A

Owner: Mr Williams, Chitterman Hills, Markfield
1 22hp Fordson Tractor, 3 Workers, 4 Horses, 12 years in occupation

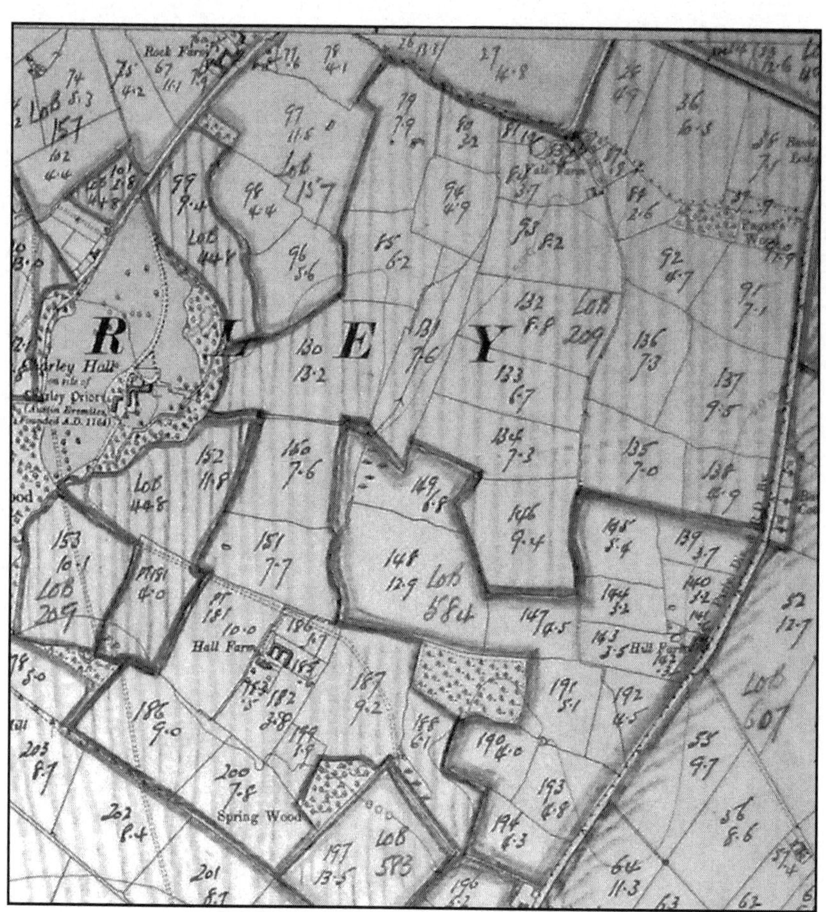

LOB 209
W Blackett
246 acres

The Return of Crops sent in by Farmer Blackett in 1941

Fill in both Forms C47/S.S. (Green) and C.47/S.S.Y. (Blue)

MINISTRY OF AGRICULTURE AND FISHERIES.

THE DEFENCE REGULATIONS, 1939, AND THE AGRICULTURAL RETURNS ORDER, 1939.

RETURN WITH RESPECT TO AGRICULTURAL LAND ON 4th JUNE, 1941.

No.	CROPS AND GRASS	Statute Acres
1	Wheat	48
2	Barley	—
3	Oats	39
4	Mixed Corn with Wheat in mixture	—
5	Mixed Corn without Wheat in mixture	17
6	Rye	—
7	Beans, winter or spring, for stock feeding	—
8	Peas, for stock feeding, not for human consumption	—
9	Potatoes, first earlies	—
10	Potatoes, main crop and second earlies	4
11	Turnips and Swedes, for fodder	3½
12	Mangolds	5
13	Sugar Beet	—
14	Kale, for fodder	—
15	Rape (or Cole)	—
16	Cabbage, Savoys, and Kohl Rabi, for fodder	4
17	Vetches or Tares FOR.HAY.	3
18	Lucerne	—
19	Mustard, for seed	—
20	Mustard, for fodder or ploughing in	—
21	Flax, for fibre or linseed	—
22	Hops, Statute Acres, not Hop Acres	—
23	Orchards, with crops, fallow, or grass below the trees	—
24	Orchards, with small fruit below the trees	—
25	Small Fruit, not under orchard trees	—
26	Vegetables for human consumption (excluding Potatoes), Flowers and Crops under Glass	—
27	All Other Crops not specified elsewhere on this return or grown on patches of less than ¼ acre	—
28	Bare Fallow	—
29	Clover, Sainfoin, and Temporary Grasses for Mowing this season	6
30	Clover, Sainfoin, and Temporary Grasses for Grazing (not for Mowing this season)	—
31	Permanent Grass for Mowing this season	38½
32	Permanent Grass for Grazing (not for Mowing this season), but excluding rough grazings	73½ +10
33	TOTAL OF ABOVE ITEMS, 1 to 32 (Total acreage of Crops and Grass, excluding Rough Grazings)	236½
34	Rough Grazings—Mountain, Heath, Moor, or Down Land, or other rough land used for grazing on which the occupier has the sole grazing rights	246

LABOUR actually employed on holding on **4th June.** The occupier, his wife, or domestic servants should not be entered.

No.			Number (in figures)
35	WHOLETIME REGULAR WORKERS — If none, write "None"	Males, 21 years old and over	3
36		Males, 18 to 21 years old	
37		Males, under 18 years old	
38		Women and Girls	
39	CASUAL (SEASONAL or PART-TIME) WORKERS	Males, 21 years old and over	
40		Males, under 21 years old	
41		Women and Girls	
		TOTAL WORKERS	3

Form No. C47/S.S.Y. 1 M.14000 4/41 (52-4851)

No.	LIVE STOCK on holding on 4th June, including any sent for sale on that or previous day		Number (in figures)
43	Cows and Heifers in milk		18
44	Cows in Calf, but not in milk		4
45	Heifers in Calf, with first Calf		7
46	Bulls being used for service		1
47	Bulls (including Bull Calves) being reared for service		
48	OTHER CATTLE	2 years old and above — Male	4
49		2 years old and above — Female	
50		1 year old and under 2 — Male	8
51		1 year old and under 2 — Female	6
52		Under 1 year old:— (a) For rearing (excluding Bull Calves being reared for service)	17
53		(b) Intended for slaughter as Calves	65 (crossed out)
54	TOTAL CATTLE and CALVES		65.
55	Steers and Heifers over 1 year old being fattened for slaughter before 30th November, 1941		
56	SHEEP OVER 1 YEAR OLD	Ewes kept for further breeding (excluding two-tooth Ewes)	28
57		Rams kept for service	1
58		Two-tooth Ewes (Shearling Ewes or Gimmers) to be put to the ram in 1941	—
59		Other Sheep over 1 year old	7
60	SHEEP UNDER 1 YEAR OLD	Ewe Lambs to be put to the ram in 1941	
61		Ram Lambs for service in 1941	
62		Other Sheep and Lambs under 1 year old	44
63	TOTAL SHEEP and LAMBS		80
64	Sows in Pig		
65	Gilts in Pig		
66	Other Sows kept for breeding		
67	Barren Sows for fattening		
68	Boars being used for service		
69	ALL OTHER PIGS (not entered above)	Over 5 months old	
70		2—5 months	
71		Under 2 months	
72	TOTAL PIGS		
73	POULTRY — If none, write "None"	Fowls over 6 months old	200
74		Fowls under 6 months old	200
75		Ducks of all ages	
76		Geese of all ages	
77		Turkeys over 6 months old	
78		Turkeys under 6 months old	
79	TOTAL POULTRY		400
80	GOATS OF ALL AGES		

No.	HORSES on holding on 4th June		Number (in figures)
81	Horses used for Agricultural Purposes (including Mares kept for breeding) or by Market Gardeners	(a) mares	2
82		(b) geldings	2
83	Unbroken Horses of 1 year old and above	(a) mares	
84		(b) geldings	
85	Light Horses under 1 year old		
86	Heavy Horses under 1 year old		
87	Stallions being used for service in 1941		
88	All Other Horses (not entered above)		
89	TOTAL HORSES		4

Farmer Blackett's Labour, Motive Power and Tenure Return. Not many farms had the use of a tractor in 1941.

1

S.F.

MINISTRY OF AGRICULTURE AND FISHERIES

AGRICULTURAL RETURN, 4th JUNE, 1941.

LABOUR ON 4th JUNE (Supplementary Questions).

			Number
	Of the REGULAR workers returned on page 1 (Questions 73—76) how many are:—		
129	WHOLE TIME FAMILY WORKERS (father, mother, son, daughter, brother, sister of occupier or his wife, but not other relations) None	male	
130		female	
	Of the CASUAL workers returned on page 1 (Questions 77—79) how many are:—		
131	EMPLOYED ON THE HOLDING THROUGHOUT THE YEAR BUT FOR ONLY PART OF THEIR TIME	male	
132		female	

MOTIVE POWER ON HOLDING ON 4th JUNE.

	FIXED OR PORTABLE ENGINES (Excluding Motor Tractors)	Number in figures	Horse Power of each
133	Water Wheels or Turbines in present use	—	
134	Water Wheels not in use, but easily repairable	—	
135	Steam Engines	—	
136	Gas Engines	—	
137	Oil or Petrol Engines	—	
138	Electric Motors	—	
139	Others (state kinds)		

	TRACTORS	Number in figures	Horse Power of each	Make or Model of Tractor
140	Wheel Tractors for field work	1	22.	Fordson
141	Wheel Tractors for stationary work only	—		—
142	Track laying Tractors			—

NOTE.—Subject to the special Question No. 134 engines or tractors that have been discarded or worn out should not be included.

RENT

ANNUAL RENT PAYABLE FOR THE HOLDING TO WHICH THIS RETURN RELATES.

		Acres	£
143	State the actual rent payable during the current year (i.e., the contract rent less any abatements but including any interest payable on improvements)		282 - 10
144	If the holding is owned by you, give the best estimate you can of the annual rental value		—
145	If the holding is partly owned and partly rented by you, state:— Acreage of land which you own and its estimated rental value	—	
146	and Acreage of land which you hold as tenant and the rent payable (for definition of rent see Question No. 143)	—	—

LENGTH OF OCCUPATION OF HOLDING.

		Years
147	How many years have you been the occupier of the holding to which this Return relates?	12
	or	
148	If you have occupied parts of the holding for different periods, give length of occupation for each	Part 1 .... acres .... years Part 2 .... acres .... years Part 3 .... acres .... years

FOR OFFICIAL USE ONLY.

The Verdict on Farmer Blackett's efforts. Page One of the Surveyor's Report here and the reverse side on the facing page..

Given a Grade A

1.

Total acreage 250·8

Arable 135/1

FARM SURVEY

County Leicestershire Code No. LR/603/210

District Loughborough Parish Charley

Name of holding Vale Farm Name of farmer W. Blackett

Address of farmer Vale Farm, Charley, Nr. Loughborough

Number and edition of 6-inch Ordnance Survey Sheet containing farmstead XXIV NW 1931

A. TENURE.

1. Is occupier tenant ... X
   owner ...
2. If tenant, name and address of owner :—
   Mr. Williams,
   Chitterman,
   Markfield
3. Is farmer full time farmer ... X
   part time farmer ...
   spare time farmer ...
   hobby farmer ...
   other type ...
   Other occupation, if any :—
4. Does farmer occupy other land ? Yes X

Name of Holding	County	Parish
1150 - 16.3		
C. Sherriff		
(m)	Corn Merchant, Wards End, Loughborough.	

5. Has farmer grazing rights over land not occupied by him ? No X
   If so, nature of such rights—

B. CONDITIONS OF FARM.

1. Proportion (%) of area on which soil is

Heavy	Medium	Light	Peaty
	100		

2. Is farm conveniently laid out ? Yes ... Moderately X No ...

	Good	Fair	Bad
3. Proportion (%) of farm which is naturally		100	
4. Situation in regard to road	X		
5. Situation in regard to railway	X		
6. Condition of farmhouse			X
Condition of buildings		X	
7. Condition of farm roads		X	
8. Condition of fences		X	
9. Condition of ditches		X	
10. General condition of field drainage	X		
11. Condition of cottages & Farmhouse		X	

	No.
12. Number of cottages within farm area	1
Number of cottages elsewhere	–
13. Number of cottages let on service tenancy	1

14. Is there infestation with :—	Yes	No
rabbits and moles		X
rats and mice		X
rooks and wood pigeons		X
other birds		X
insect pests		X
15. Is there heavy infestation with weeds ?		X

If so, kinds of weeds :—

	Yes	No
16. Are there derelict fields ?		X

If so, acreage

C. WATER AND ELECTRICITY.

Water supply :—	Pipe	Well	Roof	Stream	None
1. To farmhouse		X			
2. To farm buildings					X
3. To fields				X	

	Yes	No
4. Is there a seasonal shortage of water ?		X
Electricity supply :—		
5. Public light		X
Public power		X
Private light		X
Private power		X
6. Is it used for household purposes ?		X
Is it used for farm purposes ?		X

D. MANAGEMENT.

1. Is farm classified as A, B or C ? A
2. Reasons for B or C :—
   old age ...
   lack of capital ...
   personal failings ...

If personal failings, details :—

	Good	Fair	Poor	Bad
3. Condition of arable land	X			
4. Condition of pasture		X		

5. Use of fertilisers on :—	Adequate	To some extent	Not at all
arable land	X		
grass land	X		

Field information recorded by R.T. PAYNE

Date of recording 19th Feb 194?

This primary record completed by

Date

Form No. B496/E.I. *15940, Wt.46105/817, 2000 pads. 8/41. Wy.L.P. Gp.876.

The vital evidence here of grassland being ploughed up to grow cereals. 23.3 acres now down to oats and wheat. Farmer Blackett is doing his bit for the 10% plough-up target.

E. GENERAL COMMENTS. 1.

Farms reasonably well.

F. GRASS FIELDS PLOUGHED UP.

Field Ordnance Survey Number and edition	Parish	Crops Sown		Under W.A.E.C.'s direction	
				Yes	No
For 1940 harvest					
1150	Shepshed	16.3 acres	Oats	X	
38	Charley	7.1 "	Wheat	X	
138	"	4.9 "	"	X	
For 1941 harvest					
180	Charley	9.0 acres	Oats	X	
200	"	7.8 "	Oats and roots	X	
153	"	10.1 "	Oats	X	
133	"	6.7 "	"	X	
134	"	7.3 "	"	X	
146	"	9.4 "	"	X	
Pt. 181	"	10.0 "	"	X	

2

MR.E.BURTON, LR/192
CHARNWOOD HEATH, 135/2
COALVILLE,
LEICS.
4/NIL

Map 24 NW
Mowing Grass 3 acres
Rough pasture 2 acres
Represented on the map by the *Under 5* area
along side the Road opposite LOB 234.

Owner: Mr S W Clarke, Charnwood Lodge
2 Cows and 20 Fowls, 20 years in occupation.

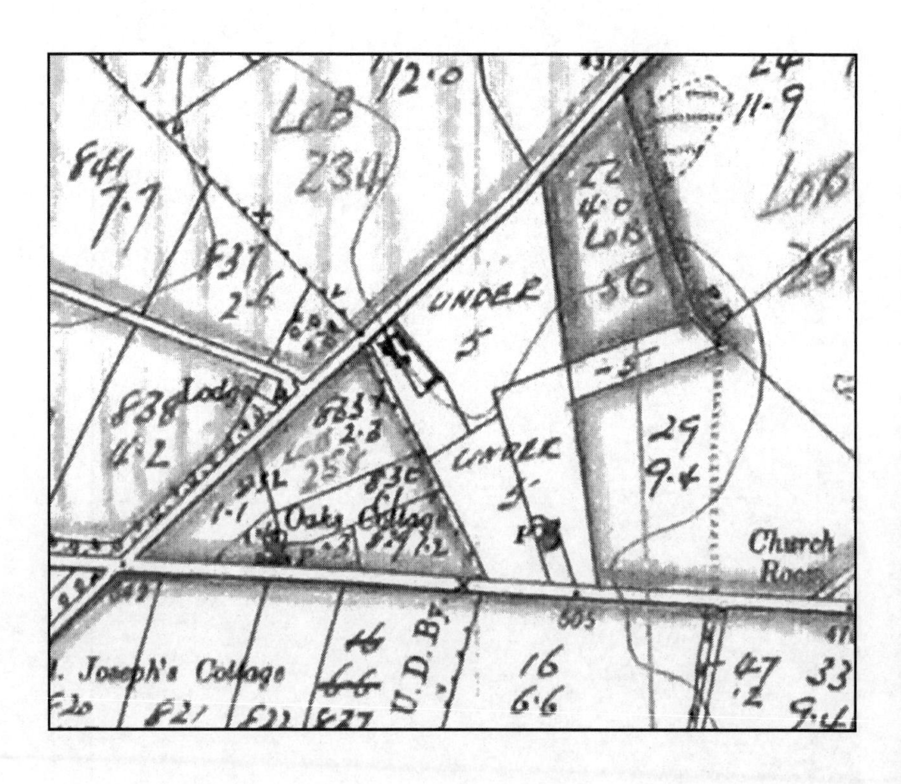

3

MR.JAMES BOWLER,
MOULT HILL,
COALVILLE,
LEICS.

LR/192
135/3

7.5/NIL

Map 24 NW
3.5 acre orchard
Represented by the other *under 5 acre* spread on the map.

Owner occupied, 21 years in occupation
33 fowls, and one 1.5 hp oil engine

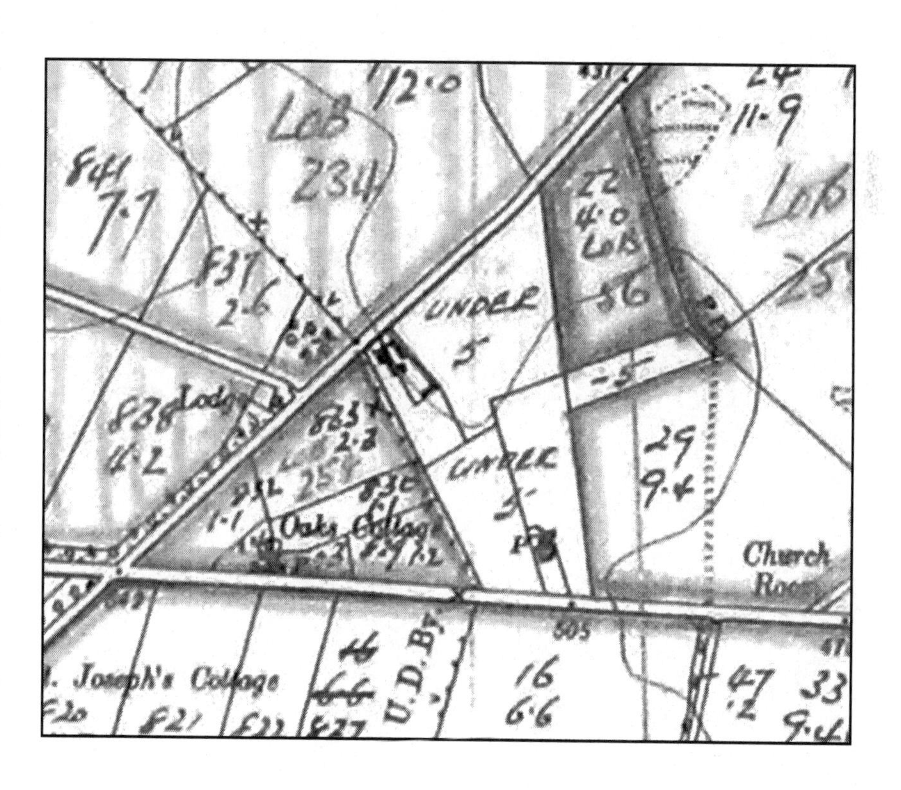

4

MESSRS.S.W.,T.C.& C.E.CLARK LR/192
CHARNWOOD LODGE, 135/4
COALVILLE,
LEICS.

20/195

Map 27 SW &
Map 24 NW
Code LOB 56 Graded A

Acreage: 195 Rough Grazing, 13.5 Arable, 10 Grass
Owners: Mr SW Clarke & Miss C E Clarke, Occupiers for 30 years
Gives valued assistance to four neighbouring farming tenants

LOB 56
S W Clark

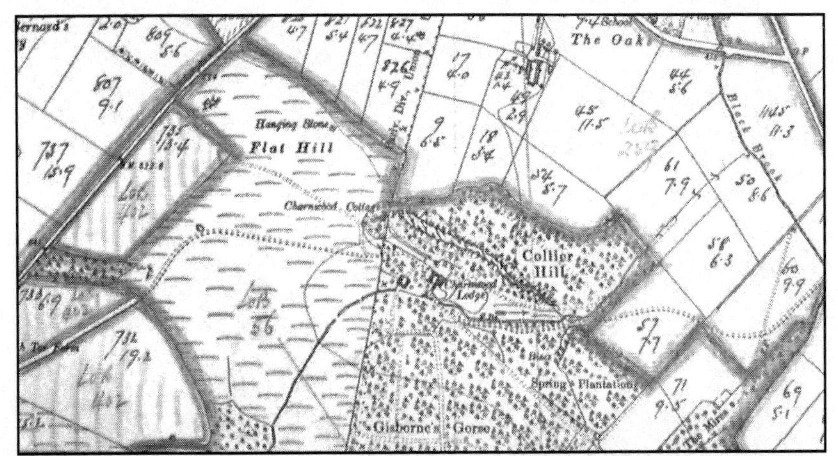

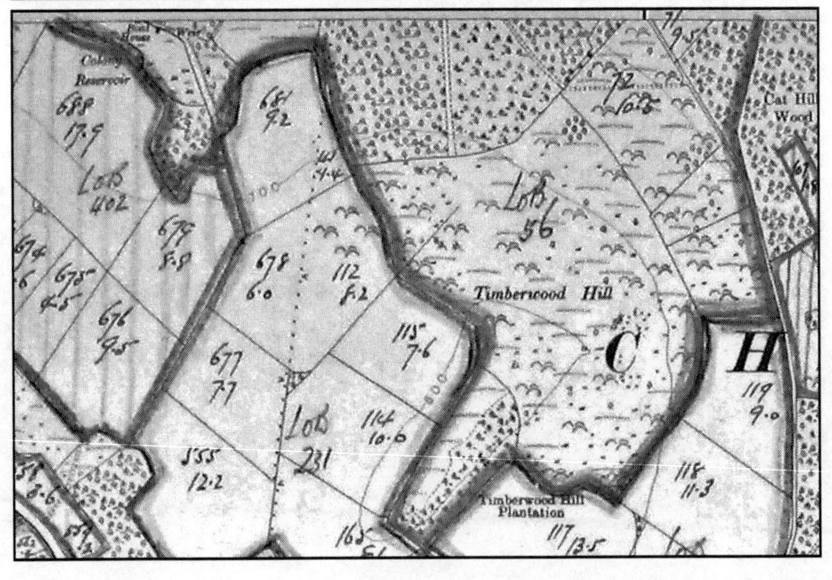

6

MR.JOHN B.MARTIN, LR/192
CHARLEY HALL, 135/6
LOUGHBOROUGH,
LEICS.
119/NIL

Map 24 NW
Map Code LOB 448
Graded B- for "no knowledge of farming"

Owner: Executors of J H Williams, c/o H Joyce, Ashby dZ.
Occupied 14 years as owner.
1 horse kept for farm use, and two others.

The record states that "the land is properly referred to as Kitchen Garden Farm, the remaining part of the Charley Estate, formerly owned by Mr Martin and recently sold to Mr Williams, of Markfield. "Mainly park land and used for grazing sheep and about two milk cows for home use".

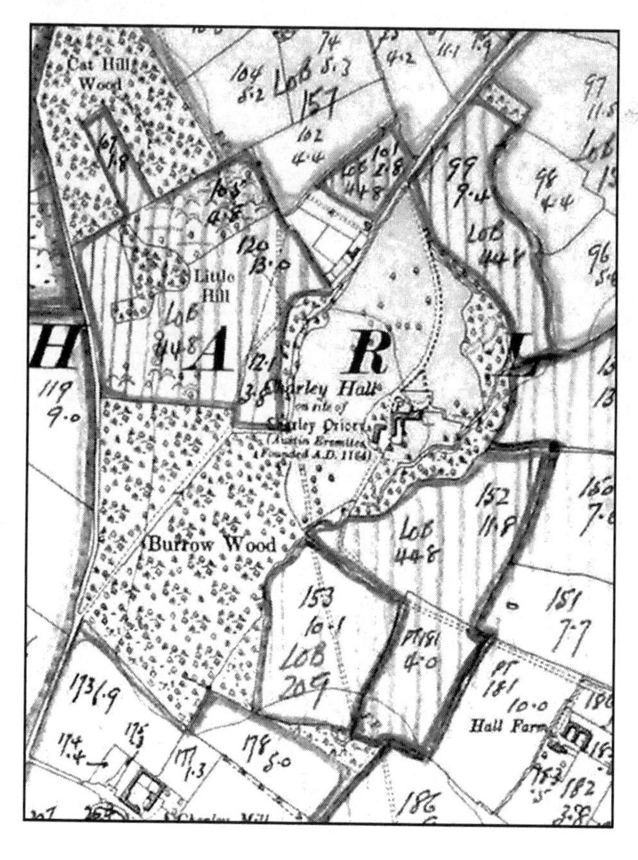

LOB 448
John
Martin

7

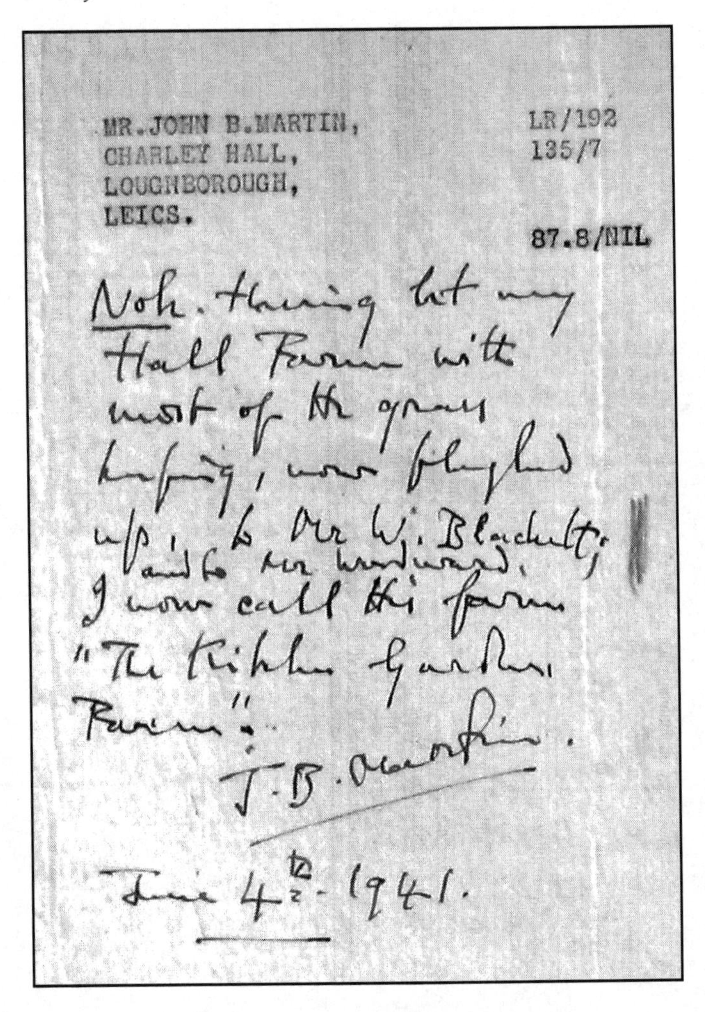

MR.JOHN B.MARTIN, LR/192
CHARLEY HALL, 135/7
LOUGHBOROUGH,
LEICS.

87.8/NIL

Note. Having let my Hall Farm with most of the grass keeping, now ploughed up, to Mr W. Blackett, and to [illegible] [illegible], I now call this farm "The Kitchen Garden Farm".

J.B. Martin.

June 4th 1941.

Map 24 NW
See map insert on previous page for Holding No. 6

Acreage:
No Rough Grazing
3 Arable
25 Grass

John Martin is here reacting to the apparent confusion in the bureaucratic mind. In future there will be just the newly named 'Kitchen Garden Farm' embracing Nos. 6 and 7, with his Hall Farm now being operated by his A-graded neighbour, Mr W Blackett, at Vale Farm.

8

MR.F.A.MACER, LR/192
BESS BAGLEY FARM, 135/8
COPT OAK,
MARKFIELD,
LEICS. 59/NIL

Map 24 NW
Map Code LOB 456

Acreage: Graded B for "little knowledge of arable farming"
No Rough Grazing
19.5 Arable
38 Grass

Owner: S Livingston, 32 Millstone Lane, Leicester
Occupied for 5 years, with no motive power and four horses.

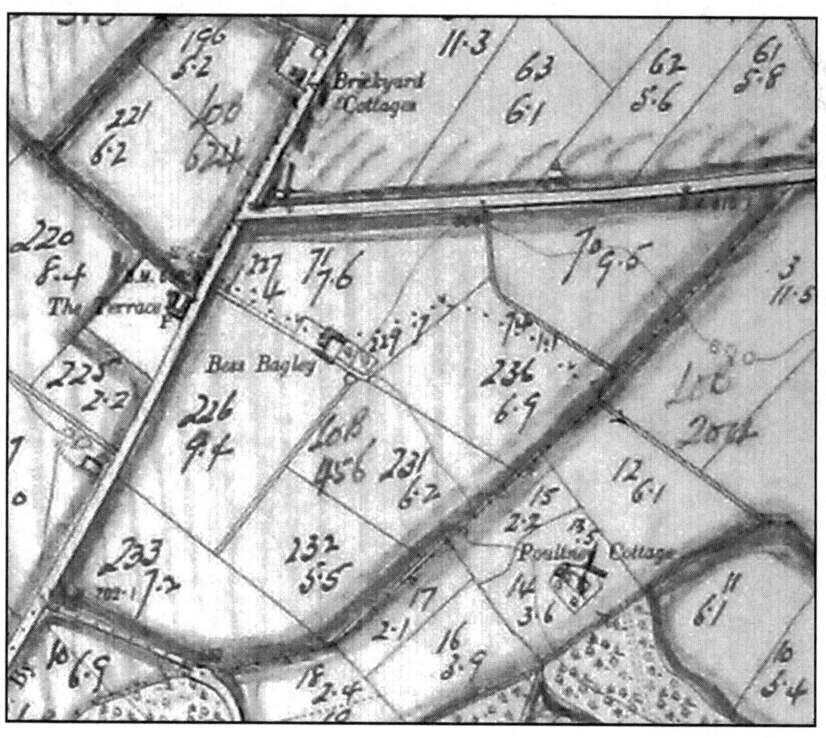

LOB 456
F A Macer

11

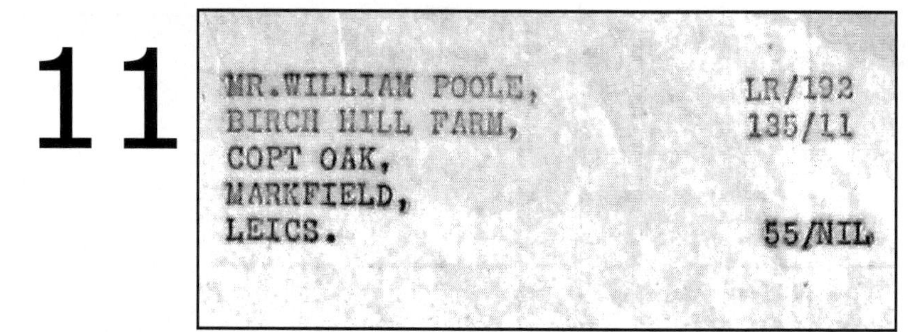

MR.WILLIAM POOLE, LR/192
BIRCH HILL FARM, 135/11
COPT OAK,
MARKFIELD,
LEICS. 55/NIL

Map 24 NW
Code: LOB 449 See commentary on Holding 12 on facing page.

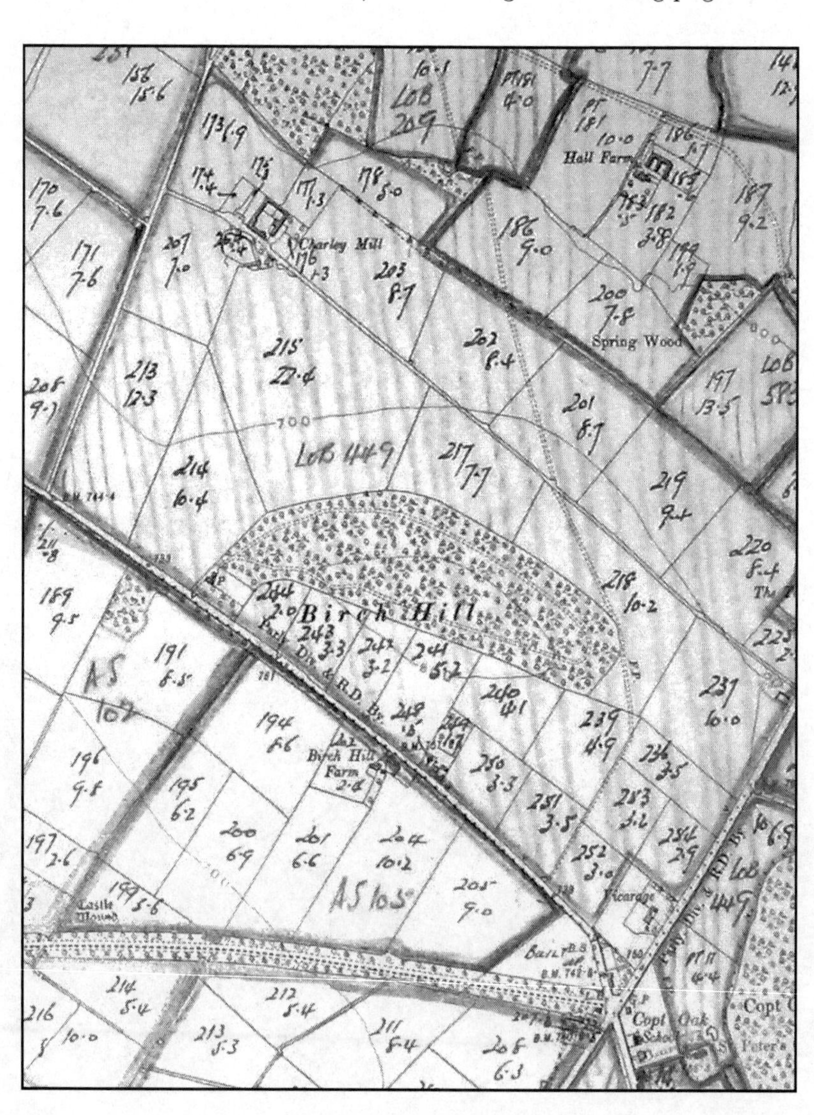

LOB 449
W Poole

12

MR.W.POOLE, LR/192
CHARLEY MILL FARM, 135/12
COPT OAK,
MARKFIELD,
LEICS. 139/NIL

Map 24 NW
Code: LOB 449

Acreage: Graded B-
No Rough Grazing
84 Arable
138.5 Grass

Graded down for "lack of initiative"

These two farms Nos 11 and 12 also seem to be heading for being joined together in the bureaucratic mind.

Ownership is spread between S W Clarke at Charnwood Lodge, the Executors of J H Williams, and the Curzon-Herrick Estates at Woodhouse.

William Poole has been the tenant for 5 years and deploys 3 small oil engines and 8 horses on the holdings.

13

MR.WILLIAM REVELL, LR/192
HIGH TOR FARM, 135/13
COALVILLE,
LEICS.
131/NIL

Map 27 SW &
Map 24 NW
Map Code: LOB 402

William Revell's holding comes from two maps which are shown on the facing page. He also has access to the free rough grazing of his landlord at Charnwood Lodge (See holding no. 4)

Acreage: Graded B-
No Rough Grazing
47 Arable
85 Grass

Owner S W Clarke at Charnwood Lodge.

Occupied for 6 years
One electric motor and 3 horses.

Graded down for "Ill Health"

13

Continued from facing page

The two maps showing the spread of the holding indicated by LOB 402, ranging over some of the highest ground of Charnwood.

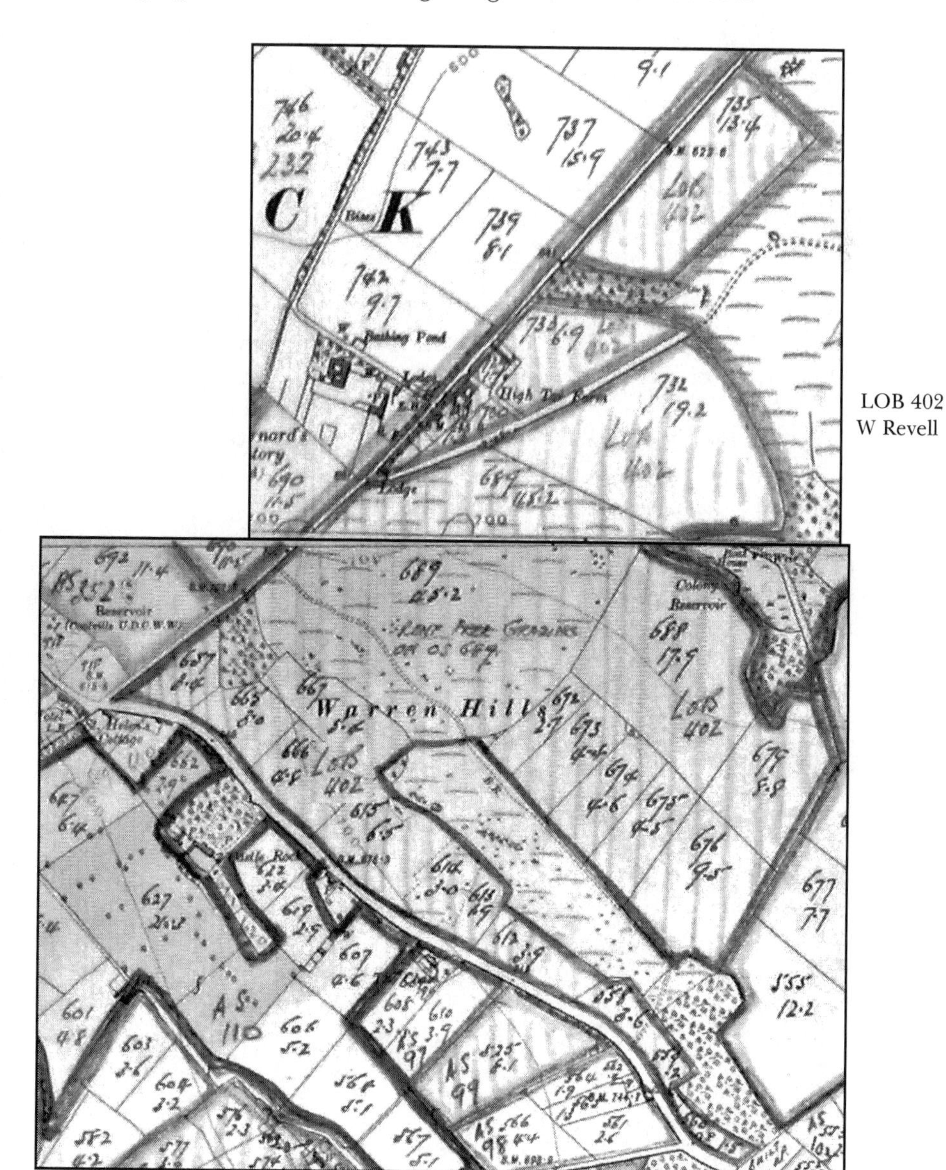

LOB 402
W Revell

14

MRS.B.RENSHAW & A.T.WRIGHT, LR/192
OAKS FARM, 135/14
CHARLEY,
LOUGHBOROUGH,
LEICS. 117/NIL

Map 27 SW
Map Code: LOB 289

Acreage: Graded A
No Rough Grazing
45 Arable
93 Grass

Owned by S W Clarke at Charnwood Lodge. Occupied by Renshaw/Wright for 6 years, following the tenancy by three generations of the Thompson family.

One 8hp electric motor and a Fordson tractor deployed, along with 6 horses.

LOB 289
Renshaw
& Wright

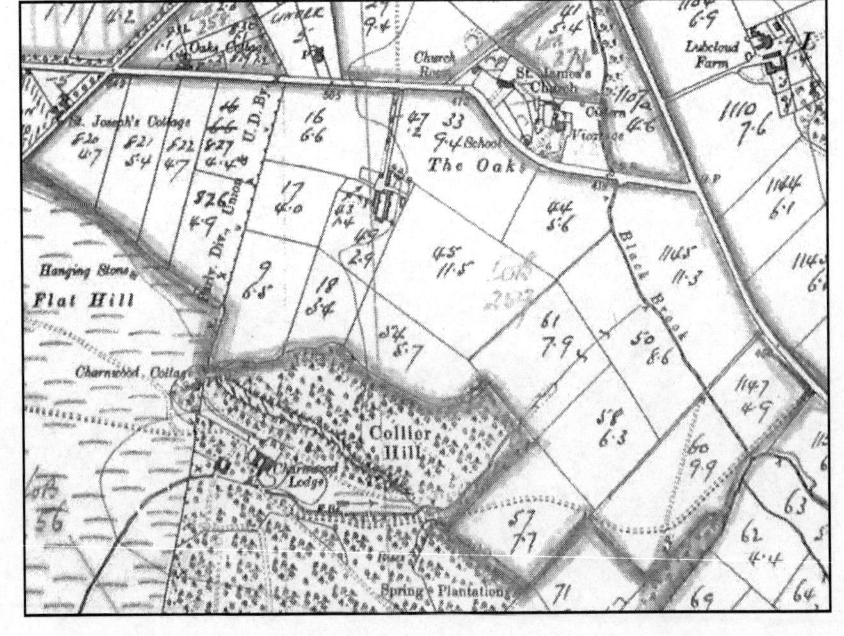

15

MESSRS.G.W.& C.R.SIDDONS, LR/192
HILL FARM, 135/15
CHARLEY,
LOUGHBOROUGH,
LEICS. 46/[illegible]

Map 24 NW
Map Code: LOB 584

Acreage: Graded B
20 Rough Grazing
27 Arable, 19 Grass

Owner: Executors of J H Williams, c/o H Joyce at Ashby dZ

The Siddons have been tenants for 8 years and run this small dairy operation in conjunction with Lower Broombriggs Farm, supplying it with dairy cows. Two working horses kept, and one for riding. One Fordson tractor deployed across both farms. Graded down for "appearing to lack arable knowledge"

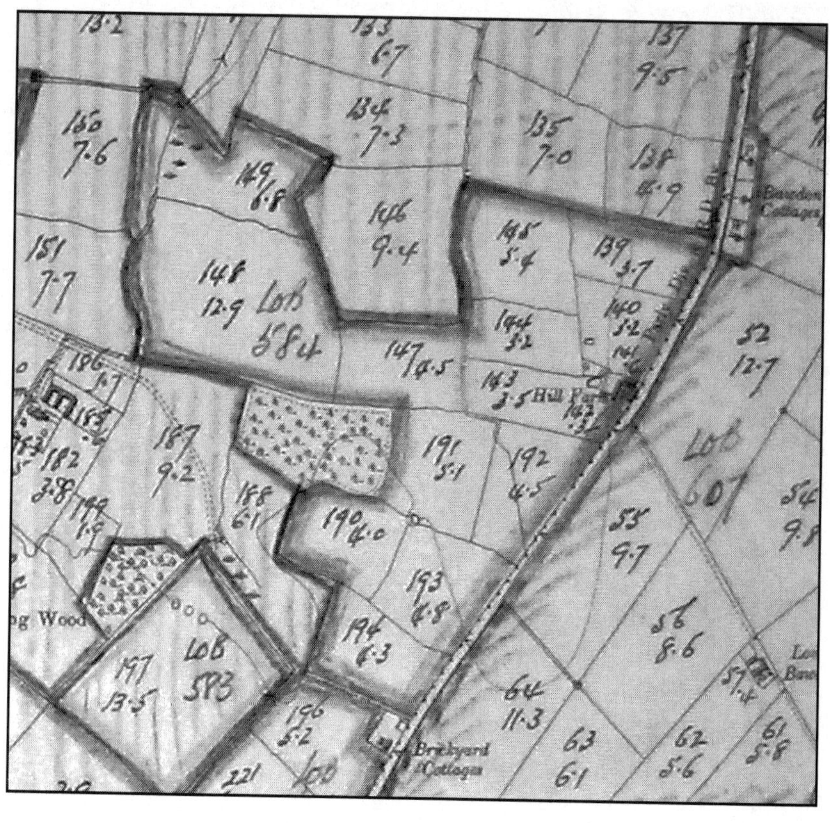

LOB 584
Siddons

16

```
THE VERY REV.                        LR/192
          FATHER SUPERIOR,           135/16
MOUNT S.BERNARD'S ABBEY,
COALVILLE,
LEICS.                               170/14
```

Map 27 SW
Map Code: LOB 232

Acreage: Graded A
14 Rough Grazing
88 Arable 86 Grass

The Survey Report shows that the Abbey has been farming for 103 years, and that its operations were right across the food production spectrum.

Two horses, two 23hp Ford tractors, two 3hp oil engines and one 1hp electric motor all figure in the listings. Only one part-time employee was listed, pointing to all the farming work being undertaken by the brothers.

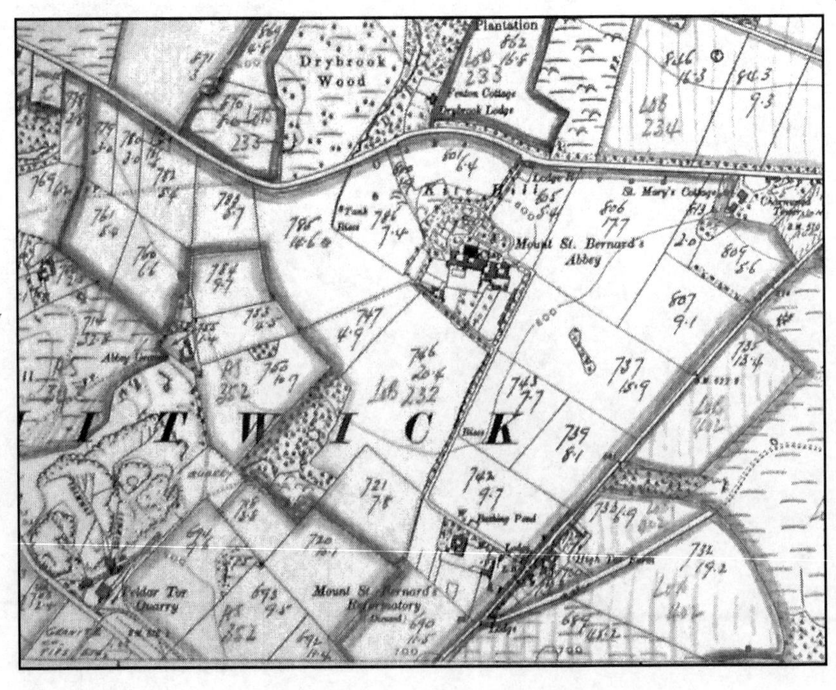

LOB 232
The
Monastery

17

MR.F.H.WOODWARD, LR/192
GREENHILL LODGE, 135/17
COALVILLE,
LEICS.

185/10

Map 24 NW
Map Code: LOB 231

Acreage:
Graded C-
10 Rough Grazing
80 Arable
97 Grass

A 20 milk-cow operation

Owner: S W Clarke at Charnwood Lodge.

Five horses used, plus one 4hp electric motor

Tenant for 14 years. Two sisters help on the farm.

The inspector R T Payne gives this farm the worst possible grade, and comments that "the farmer appears to lack all knowledge of arable farming".

LOB 231
F H
Woodward

19

The facsimile of the Addressograph Plate does not appear in the records at Kew. Below is the detail on the holding as set out on the Survey Report.

19 **FARM SURVEY**

Total acreage

Arable

County Leicestershire Code No.

District Loughborough Parish Ulverscroft

Name of holding Chitterman Hills Name of farmer C.H. & F.O. Sherriff

Address of farmer Chitterman Hills, Markfield, Nr. Leicester.

Number and edition of 6-inch Ordnance Survey Sheet containing farmstead XXIV N.W., S.W., N.E. & S.E.,

Map 24 NW SW NE & SE
Map Code: LOB 213 See also facing page

Acreage: Graded A
120 Arable
183 Grass

Professional farm operator also of Brook farm, Loughborough, picking up several arable holdings in the forest area not capable of being worked by previous tenants. No tractors listed.

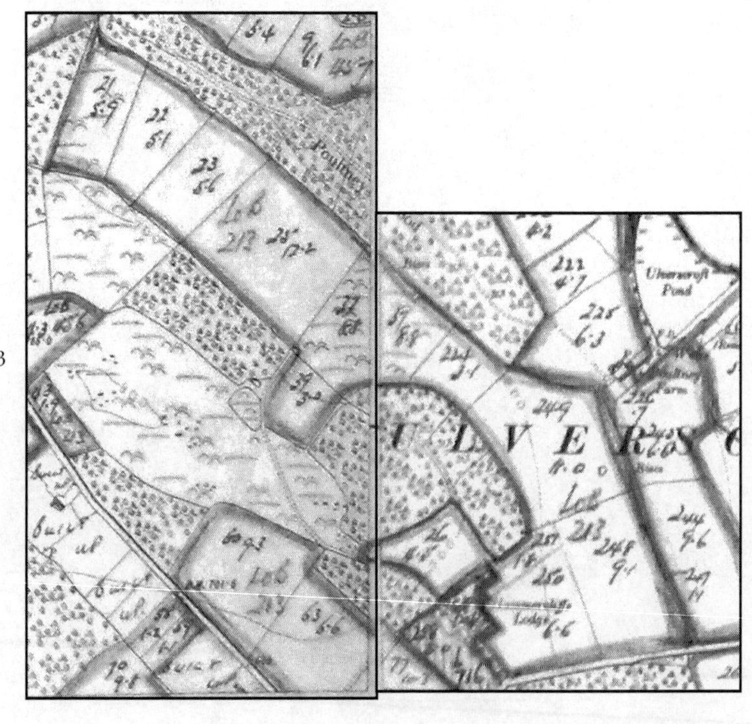

LOB 213
Sherriff

19 Continued LOB 213 from facing page

Owners include:
L T Lillingston, Ulvescroft Cott.
CC Jones, High Robey, Markf.
Mr Livingston, Millstone Lane
Leicester
D Elliott, Newtown Linford.

LOB 213
Sherriff

20

MR.STANLEY WALKER, LR/192
DRY BROOK FARM, 135/20
COALVILLE,
LEICS.
95/9

Map 27 SW
Map Code: LOB 233

Acreage: Graded B+
9 Rough Grazing
27 Arable
49 Grass

Marked down to B+ as being short of capital.

Owner: E M P de Lisle of Garendon

Tenant for 4 years

5 horses kept, and no motive power listed.

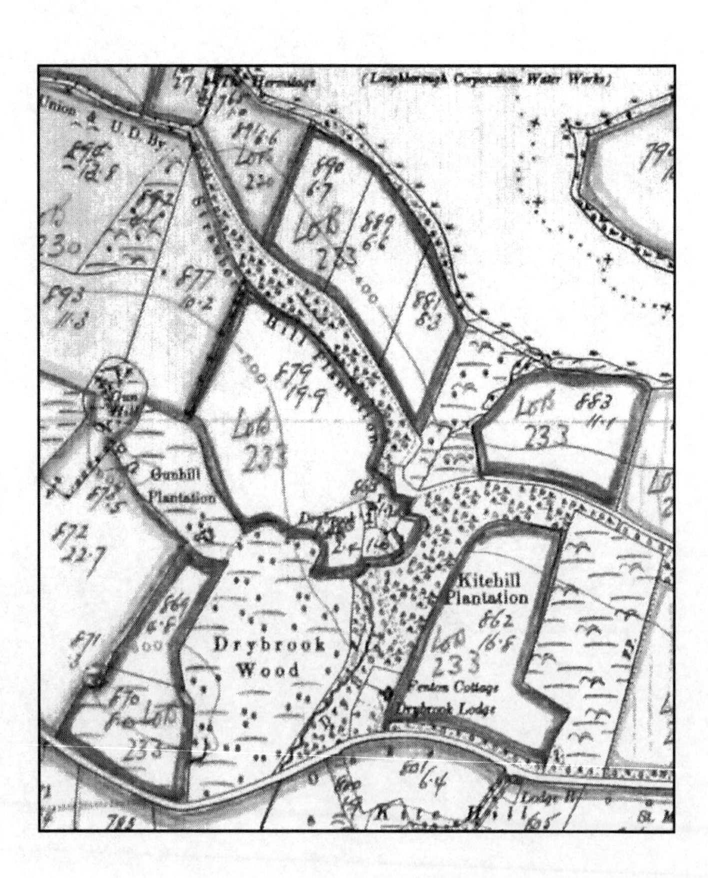

LOB 233
Stanley
Walker

21

MR.GEORGE WOOLLISCROFT, LR/192
ONE BARROW LODGE, 135/21
COALVILLE,
LEICS.

127.5/20.5

Map 27 SW
Map Code: LOB 234

Acreage: Graded A-
20 Rough Grazing
45 Arable
85 Grass

Owner: E M P de Lisle, Garendon Hall. Tenanted for 4 years.

"33 cows producing 50 gallons of milk per day. Forest farm which is well farmed", was the report.
No tractors, 6 horses

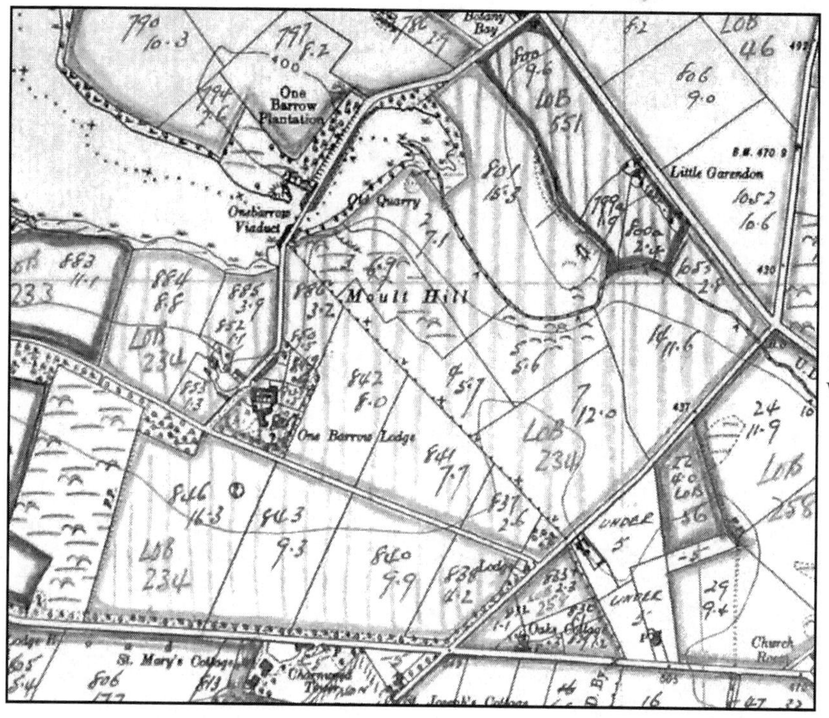

LOB 234
Wolliscroft

22

MR.J.J.BLACKETT, LR/192
CHARLEY KNOLL FARM, 135/22
LOUGHBOROUGH,
LEICS.

160.2/NIL

Map 27 SW
Map Code: LOB 498

Acreage: Graded A-
No Rough Grazing
57 Arable
125 Grass

Dairy farm managed by William Blackett of Vale Farm, the son of the occupier, actually Mrs M A Blackett.

Owner: C Sherriff, Wards End, Loughborough. Tenanted for 40 years

One International 10/20hp tractor, one 2.5hp oil engine, and 5 horses deployed.

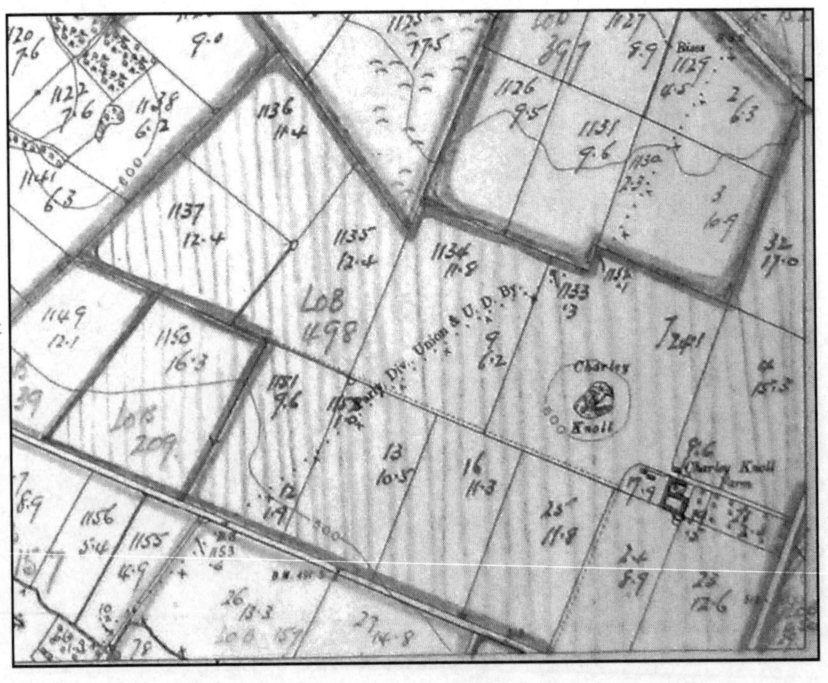

LOB 498
W Blackett

23

MR.A.E.BARKER,
BURLEIGH FARM,
NANPANTAN,
LOUGHBOROUGH,
LEICS.

LR/192
185/23

55/NIL

Map 24 NE
Map Code: LOB 443

Acreage: Graded C
No Rough Grazing
32 Arable
22 Grass

Owner-occupier of 22 years marked down to Grade C for "lack of organising ability and more land than can be adequately managed".

LOB 443
A E Barker

24

MR.GEORGE POOLE, LR/192
WHITTLE HILL FARM, 135/24
LOUGHBOROUGH,
LEICS.

104/6

Map 27 SE
Map Code: LOB 284

Acreage: Graded C
6 Rough Grazing
48 Arable 58 Grass

Marked down to C for "lack of capital and initiative"

Owner: Curzon-Herrick Estates of Beaumanor. Tenant for 21 years
Deploying 3 horses

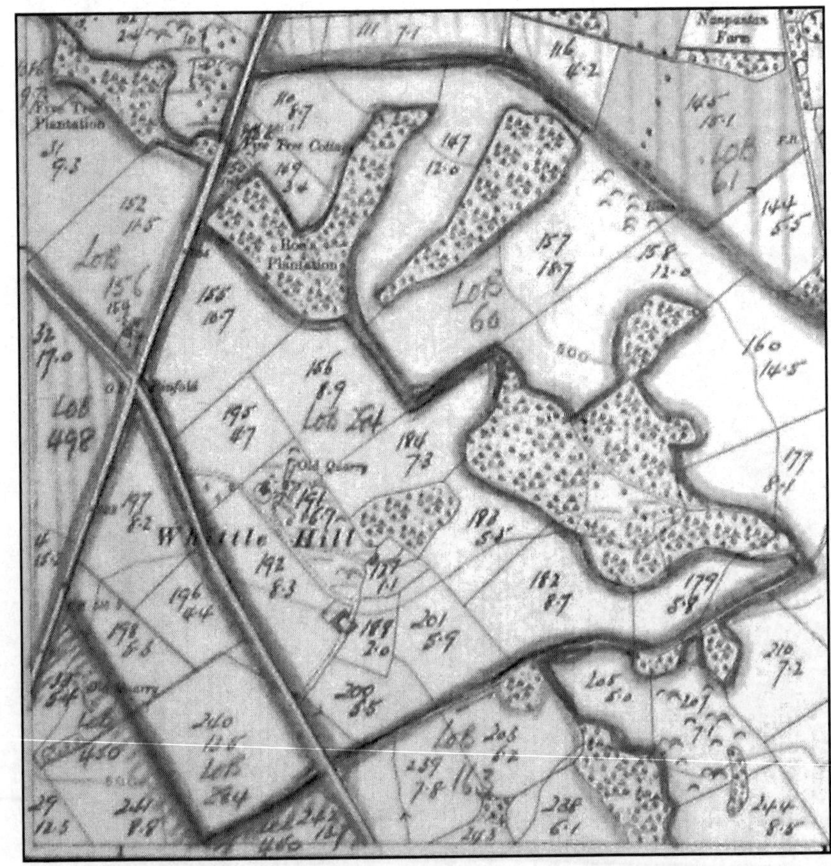

LOB 284
George
Poole

25

MR.J.C.SMITH,
BILLA BARRA,
STANTON-U-BARDON,
LEICESTER.

LR/192
135/25
BILLA BARRA

12.5/NIL

Map 24 NW
MapCode: LOB 624

Acreage: Graded B
No Rough Grazing
6.2 Arable
5.2 Grass

Owner: Executors of J H Smith,c/o H Joyce at Ashby dZ. Tenant for 3 years

Marked down to Grade B for "lack of time to spend on the holding because of full-time occupation as a farm worker".

"Land is used to graze store beast, down calving heifers and sheep".

I gelding deployed

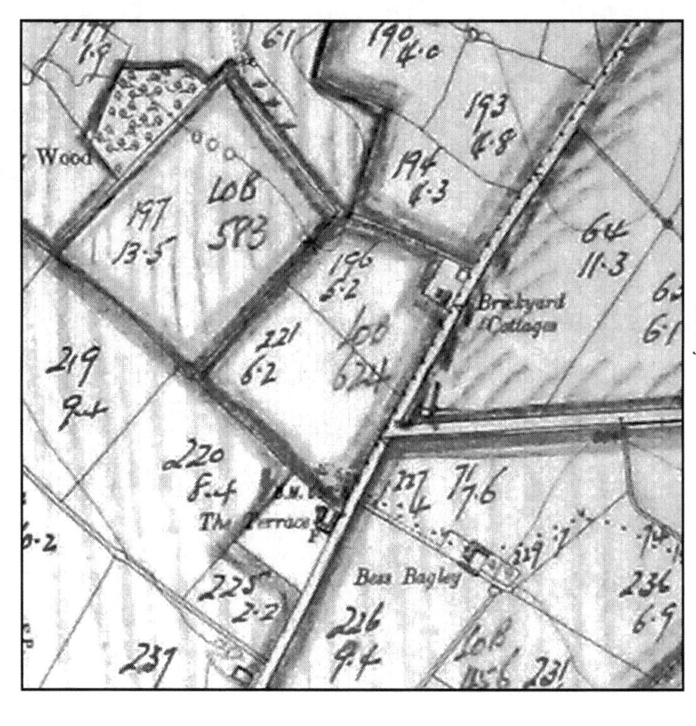

LOB 624
J C Smith

26

MR.L.BARKER,JNR., LR/192
BURLEIGH FARM, 135/26
NANPANTAN,
LOUGHBOROUGH,
LEICS. 63/NIL

Map 27 SE
Map Code: LOB ?397

Acreage:
No Rough Grazing
No Arable
63 Grass

No Farm Survey Return. Data & Map assumed

Tenant for 10 years
1 horse deployed

LOB 397
L Barker
Jnr

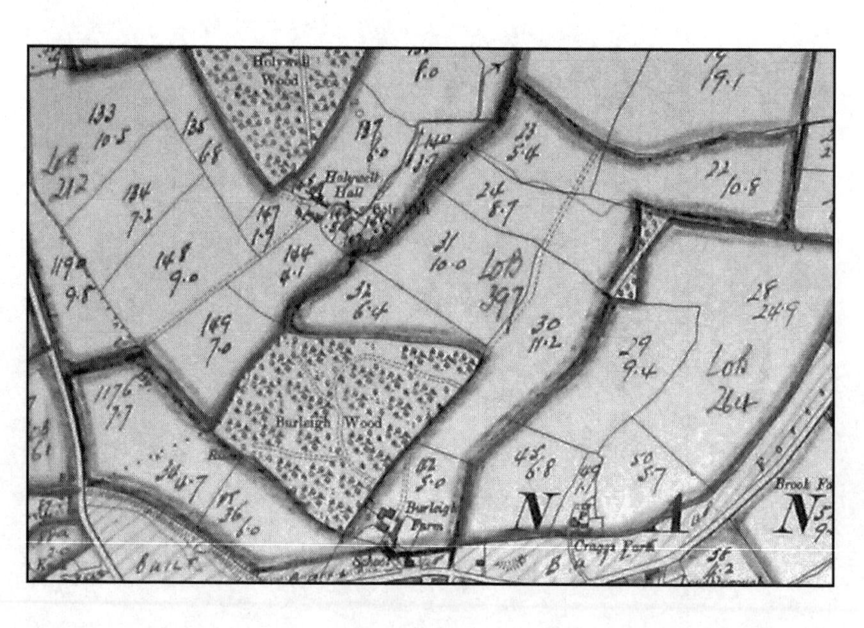

27

Mr. J. Renshaw, LR/192
The Oaks Cottage, 135/27
Charley,
Loughborough, 44/NIL
Leics.

Map 27 SW
Map Code: LOB 258

Acreage: Graded B
No Rough Grazing
No Arable
45 Grass

Grading reflects lack of capital

Owner: P Paget, through Wooleys & Noel, Rectory Place, Loughborough

John Renshaw, tenant for 4 years, described as "part-timer with another occupation of producer retailer". 1 horse deployed.

" Most of the fields are on rock and are not suitable for breaking up".

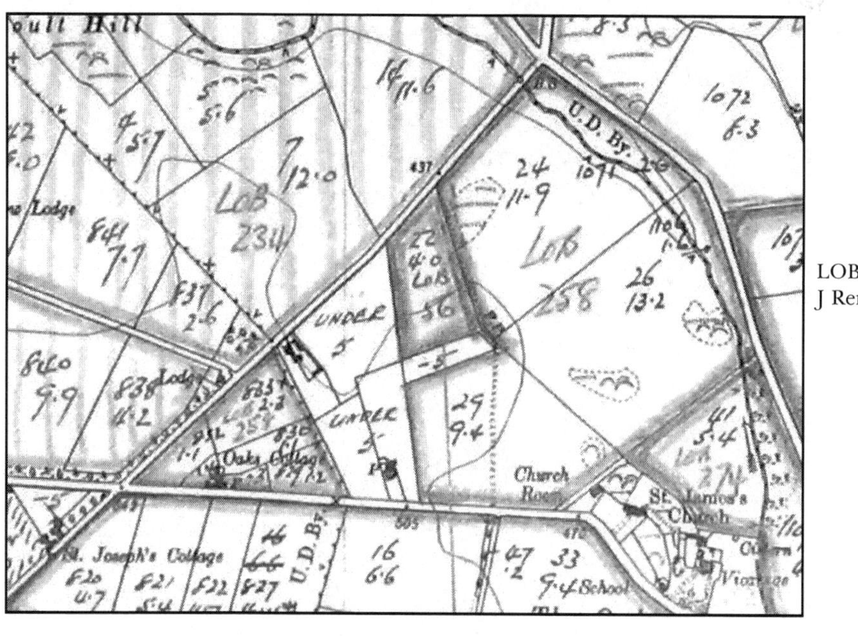

LOB 258
J Renshaw

28

Mr. Charles Webb,
Poultney Cottage Farm,
Ulverscroft,
Markfield,
Leicester.

LR/192
135/28.
from 135/19.

Your Acreage last year was Crops & Grass / Rough Grazings

Map 24 NW
Map Code: LOB 204

Acreage: Graded C
No Rough Grazing
33 Arable
24 Grass

Grading reflects lack of capital and "little knowledge of arable farming"

Owner: S H R Livingstone
32 Millstone Lane, Leicester

Tenant for 7 years with 2 horses deployed.

LOB 204
Charles
Webb

A Summary of the data on the 24 Farms within the Charley Parish No. 135

1941 Farm Table

MAF No.	Farm Name	Parish	OS Map	LOB	MAF Grade	Farmer	Owner	Acres	Years On
135/									
1	Vale Farm	Charley	24NW	209	A	William Blackett	Williams, Chitterman	246	12
2	Charnwood Heath	Charley	24NW			Ernest Burton		3	20
3	Moult Hill Orchard	Charley	24NW			James Bowler		3.5	21
4	Charnwood Lodge	Charley	24NW-27SW	56	A	SW, TC, CE Clarke	SW & CE Clarke	217	30
6	Charley Hall	Charley Hall	24NW	448	B-	John B Martin	John B Martin	37.5	14
7	Kirkham Gardens	Charley Hall	24NW			John B Martin	John B Martin	28	20
8	Bess Bagley	Ulverscroft	24NW	456	B	F A Macer	S Livingstone	57.5	5
12	Charley Mill	Charley	24NW	449	B-	William Poole	Clarke/Williams/Herrick	222.5	5
11	Birch Hill	Copt Oak	24NW	449	B-	William Poole	Clarke/Williams/Herrick	do	5
13	High Tor	Charley	24NW-27SW	402	B-	William Revell	SW & CE Clarke	132	6
14	Oaks Farm	Charley	27SW	289	A	Mrs B Renshaw/AT Wright	SW & CE Clarke	138	6
15	Hill Farm	Charley	24NW	584	B	GW & CR Siddons	Williams	66	8
16	MSB Abbey	Charley	27SW	232	A	Father Superior	MSB	188	103
17	Greenhill Lodge	Charley	24NW	231	C-	FH Woodward	SW & CE Clarke	187	14
18	Rock Farm	Charley	24NW-27SW	157	A	JR Woodward	John B Martin	157	6
19	Chitterman Hills	Ulverscroft	24 All	213	A	CH & FC Sherriff	Livingstone/Jones/Elliott	303	1
20	Dry Brook	Charley	27SW	233	B+	Stanley Walker	EMP deLisle	85	4
21	One Barrow Lodge	Charley	27SW	234	A-	George Wooliscroft	EMP deLisle	150	4
22	Charley Knoll	Charley	27SW	498	A-	M A Blackett	C Sherriff	182	40
23	Bawdon Cottage	Woodhouse	24NE	443	C	A E Barker	(also at Burleigh Farm)	54	22
24	Whittle Hill	Woodhouse	27SE	284	C	George Poole	Curzon Herrick Estate	112	21
25	Billa Barra	Charley	24NW	624	B	J C Smith	J H Williams	11.4	3
26	Burleigh Farm	Nanpantan	27SE	397		L Barker jnr	(also at Bawdon Cottage)	63	10
27	Oaks Cottage	Charley	27SW	258	B	John Renshaw	P Paget	45	4
28	Poultney Cottage	Ulverscroft	24NW	204	C	Charles Webb	S Livingstone	57	7
							Total Acres	2745.4	

The supervision of the Charley Farms was undertaken by the Leicestershire County War Agricultural Committee. Here is a copy of the official embossed record of the appointment of Howard Coltman Esq, of Burleigh Hall to that Committee. Mr Coltman would become the chairman of the Loughborough Sub-Committee of the County body, through which the detailed oversight of Charley farms was delegated.

DEFENCE OF THE REALM.

WAR AGRICULTURAL EXECUTIVE COMMITTEE

County of Leicester.

The Minister of Agriculture and Fisheries hereby appoints Howard Coltman Esq., of Burleigh Hall, Loughborough, to be a member of the War Agricultural Executive Committee for the administrative County of Leicester.

The Minister may at any time revoke this appointment.

IN WITNESS whereof the Official Seal of the Minister of Agriculture and Fisheries is hereunto affixed this nineteenth day of July nineteen hundred and forty.

Secretary.

The schedule of members of that Loughborough Sub Committee that would meet most weeks in the offices of the National Farmers' Union in Ashby Road, Loughborough.

County ........LEICESTERSHIRE........

PARTICULARS OF DISTRICT SUB-COMMITTEES

District ........LOUGHBOROUGH........

How defined ....PETTY SESSIONAL DIVISIONS........
(R.D.C. or other boundaries)

Chairman ....H. COLTMAN, ESQ., BURLEIGH HALL, LOUGHBOROUGH.

Members ....W. H. BRICKWOOD, MANOR FARM, COTES, LOUGHBOROUGH
H. GORE-BROWNE, BROOMBRIGGS, WOODHOUSE EAVES, NR. LOUGHBOROUGH.
W. H. MARSH, BURTON BANDALLS, LOUGHBOROUGH.
A. F. STANILAND, MANOR FARM, LONG WHATTON, LOUGHBOROUGH.
H. A. SWAIN, WHATTON FIELDS, LONG WHATTON, LOUGHBOROUGH.
E. E. WELLS, THE MOORS, KEGWORTH, DERBY.
C. Boucher, 117. Nottingham Road, Leicester.

The County War Office was in Friar Lane, where the addressograph plates and machine were kept. Here is the reverse side of the Crops Return Form bearing the return address.

FOLD HERE

ON HIS MAJESTY'S SERVICE.

10 JNE 1941

OFFICIAL PAID

The Executive Officer,

Leicestershire War Agricultural Executive Committee,

7, Friar Lane,

Leicester.

FOLD HERE FIRST

Ministry of Agriculture and Fisheries, St. Annes-on-Sea.

TUCK IN THIS FLAP

FOLD HERE